Creation to New Creation:

Daily Readings and Reflections from Genesis for Lent

David Gerrard

Creation to New Creation

Creation to New Creation: Daily Readings and Reflections from Genesis for Lent

Copyright © 2023 David Gerrard

All rights reserved. This book or any portion thereof may not be reproduced or used in any manner whatsoever without the express written permission of the publisher except for the use of brief quotations in a book review of scholarly journal.

First Printing: 2023

All biblical references taken from NIVUK unless otherwise stated.

ISBN: 9798375076133

DEDICATION

*For my Dad,
Wayne Gerrard.
The first father I ever knew and the one who made it
so easy to believe in a perfect heavenly father.
We miss you and we love you.*

Creation to New Creation

Contents

	Page
Foreword	
by Bishop Nick Baines	x
Introduction	1
Week of Ash Wednesday	
Ash Wednesday	
Genesis 1:11-13	4
Thursday after Ash Wednesday	
Genesis 1:27-31	7
Friday after Ash Wednesday	
Genesis 2:7; 3:19b	10
Saturday after Ash Wednesday	
Genesis 2:2-3	13

Creation to New Creation

Week 1

  Monday
    Genesis 3:8-13   16
  Tuesday
    Genesis 3:14-15, 21   20
  Wednesday
    Genesis 4:3b-8   23
  Thursday
    Genesis 6:11-13; 7:11b-12   26
  Friday
    Genesis 8:1-5   29
  Saturday
    Genesis 6:9b; 9:20-23   32

Week 2

  Monday
    Genesis 11:1-9   36
  Tuesday
    Genesis 12:1-3   40
  Wednesday
    Genesis 12:1   43

Thursday
- *Genesis 12:3* — 46

Friday
- *Genesis 15:7-18* — 49

Saturday
- *Genesis 16:1-4* — 52

Week 3

Monday
- *Genesis 16:6-10* — 55

Tuesday
- *Genesis 17:5* — 59

Wednesday
- *Genesis 18:1-8* — 63

Thursday
- *Genesis 18:18-19* — 67

Friday
- *Genesis 19:15-17, 26* — 70

Saturday
- *Genesis 12:10-13, 17-19; 20:1-3, 9* — 74

Creation to New Creation

Week 4

Monday
Genesis 18:9-15; 21:2-7   78

Tuesday
Genesis 22:1-13, 16-17   82

Wednesday
Genesis 23:1-4; 24:1-4   87

Thursday
Genesis 24:61-67   91

Friday
Genesis 26:1, 7-11   95

Saturday
Genesis 27:1-10, 18-19   99

Week 5

Monday
Genesis 27:35-36a, 41   103

Tuesday
Genesis 27:42-44   107

Wednesday
Genesis 28:10-16   111

Creation to New Creation

Thursday
> *Genesis 29:16-18, 22-30*   114

Friday
> *Genesis 32:24-28*   118

Saturday
> *Genesis 34:1-4, 8-10, 14-15, 24-25*   121

Holy Week

Holy Monday
> *Genesis 37:26-28*   125

Holy Tuesday
> *Genesis 39:1-5a, 6b-8a, 11-15, 19-23*   128

Holy Wednesday
> *Genesis 42:21-24*   132

Maundy Thursday
> *Genesis 49:8-12*   136

Good Friday
> *Genesis 50:15-17*   139

Holy Saturday
> *Genesis 50:18-21*   142

Easter Week

Easter Monday
John 20:1, 11, 14-16   145

Easter Tuesday
Colossians 3:1-4, 9b-14   148

Easter Wednesday
Philippians 1:1-6   151

Easter Thursday
Galatians 3:6-9, 16, 26-29   154

Easter Friday
Romans 4:13-16   157

Easter Saturday
Revelation 21:1-5a   160

Acknowledgements   163

Foreword
By The Rt Revd Nick Baines,
Bishop of Leeds

The beginning of human freedom is to recognise and come to terms with who and how we are. Human beings are mortal - born of the dust of the earth … to which we shall one day return; we inhabit a contingent world over which we do not have control; and we can be seen through.

For some people, being 'seen through' brings only fear. As David Gerrard illustrates in a variety of ways in this intriguing book, we realise that we are 'naked' - transparent - and then have a choice to make: to live freely without fear of being known, or to expend considerable energy in an attempt to create an image - a persona - that improves on the reality.

The book of Genesis was probably written by and for a people who languished in exile. The world had become disordered. Everything that spoke to them of God and their identity as children of God had been stripped away, leaving them to the mockery of their conquerors. After all, it is some 'god' who leaves his people abandoned and humiliated in the land of the heathens, isn't it? But, this will chime with a lot of readers who find life challenging

Creation to New Creation

and out of their ultimate control. Where is God when our own lives get stripped back?

Well, David's book gently and kindly opens up new possibilities. Being known by God allows us to lose our fear: of failure, of nakedness, of fear itself. The story told in Genesis is of a people who try to answer the question: what does God look like? They compromise and struggle; they get stuff wrong; they try to be faithful, but sometimes become inhumane in the attempt. They shape God in a particular image, but find that this same God surprises them with love and justice and mercy and the freedom to start again.

This book is a gift for those who wish to read afresh the Genesis story and reflect on its lessons for us who live in a different world three thousand years later. It offers an invitation for individuals or groups to read together, open up together, and tell their own stories together ... knowing that this same God has created them, loves them, redeems them, and opens to them a future coloured by grace.

BISHOP NICK BAINES

Introduction

To be honest, Lent and the book of Genesis may not immediately seem like natural partners.
Lent is a time of preparing to celebrate the events of Holy Week, a forty day period of reflection, repentance and rumination. Genesis on the other hand is a long-winding story, full of ups and downs, twists and turns and frankly, quite a few odd bits! It covers everything from the creation of the universe to people being turned into pillars of salt.
I've always kind of enjoyed Lent. I enjoy how it starts in the winter, with dark long nights and frozen windscreens, slowly builds up to spring, with the first daffodils and the long awaited sun on my back. I value the invitation to once again examine my life with God and whether I have allowed myself to drift away from my promise to serve him. A kind of spiritual MOT. It's a time to honestly reflect on myself and face up to the areas of my life that are not what I would hope them to be.
Which is actually why I also love Genesis.
Genesis is one of the oldest books in the Bible. Exactly when it was written is a matter of debate and it may well have been edited together in the form we have it now

much later. It describes a very ancient world. A world vastly different from the world we know and live in. A world of tribes, violence and sacrifices. A world of slavery and patriarchal dominance. In many ways it's a world about as far removed from the world we know as it is possible to conceive.

Yet when I read it I don't find it foreign at all. I find it shockingly relevant. The characters jump off the page as real people with real flaws - just like me. Their relationship to God is not one of constant obedience and faith, but one of doubts and mess.

Lent is about admitting our own faults and Genesis is all about the faults of human beings. Whether that's human beings millennia ago, or human beings now. Human beings who are both capable of awe-inspiring love and devastating evil. Who are both made in the divine image and made from the dust. Lent is about being honest with ourselves about this fact.

Each day, from Ash Wednesday through to the week following Easter, there is a short reading from Genesis followed by a reflection and a prayer. I invite you to pause each day and dwell with me on what we read and reflect on how this is relevant to your life and our world today. I suspect you'll be surprised at just how apt Genesis continues to be.

Finally, I wrote this short Lenten reflection with the idea of supporting St Catherine's Church in Wakefield, of which I am fortunate enough to be the vicar.

St Catherine's does incredible work loving and supporting the city of Wakefield. We run initiatives tackling food poverty, helping with mental health illness and supporting the elderly. However, the cost of living crisis is making it increasingly difficult to continue this vital work. While the primary purpose of this work is to help people reflect on scripture together, if there were to be any profits they will all go to the work of St Catherine's. If you are able to give any extra we would be so grateful and I can promise you it will be used to help those who need it most. You can give by going to https://givealittle.co/campaigns/3ef12aac-2ea1-41ce-84b9-3074ebbd4e0a or scanning the QR code below.

Now, on with the journey.

Creation to New Creation

Ash Wednesday

11 Then God said, 'Let the land produce vegetation: seed-bearing plants and trees on the land that bear fruit with seed in it, according to their various kinds.' And it was so. 12 The land produced vegetation: plants bearing seed according to their kinds and trees bearing fruit with seed in it according to their kinds. And God saw that it was good. 13 And there was evening, and there was morning – the third day.
Genesis 1:11-13

Lent begins with Ash Wednesday, launching a time of repentance and reflection. It is a time set aside in the Church's calendar to engage in the brave task of seeking to shine the pure light of Christ into the darkest corners of our lives. To look into our psyches and honestly ask ourselves where we have failed to be directed by love and instead have, often unthinkingly, chosen to be directed by selfishness, fear or bitterness. A time of honesty about our own failures. Therefore, it may seem strange to begin Lent in the creation story. After all, didn't God make the world perfect? A paradise?

If you're like me, the word perfect tends to make me think of something that cannot be improved, and is therefore unchanging and static. Like a sublime renaissance painting or a beautiful, white, marble statue. Breathtaking. Awe-inspiring. But eternally unvarying. Therefore, it might come as a surprise to find that God does not describe the creation as perfect, but as 'good'. Maybe this is because the creation was changeable?

In Genesis 1 God creates light, land, plants and animals. However, when he does so he creates them as the beginning, not the end, of a journey. For example, God does not say, 'Let us produce vegetation'. Instead he says, 'Let the land produce vegetation.' God creates the land with the ability to grow new things, to develop and change and advance. Likewise, birds, animals and humans are told to be fruitful and increase in number.

> The creation in Genesis 1 is not a static, unchanging, perfection, but a good, dynamic, pulsating creation brimming with possibilities and potential.

Instead of creating each individual fish God creates fish that can create fish! The creation in Genesis 1 is not a static, unchanging, perfection, but a good, dynamic, pulsating creation brimming with possibilities and potential.

God does not create a fixed unchanging world, but something that will develop, grow and adapt. He doesn't paint a perfect piece of art, he produces the first chapter of a story that could and will go in any number of directions.

Creation to New Creation

The world was made good, not perfect.
Seen in this light, Genesis 1 might just be the perfect start to Lent. Lent is a time of repentance, but it is not an unchanging repentance. It is not dwelling on failings and sin just so we can wallow in our own darkness and bitterness. Lent is a journey. A journey of clearing out the clutter and spring cleaning the rooms of our minds. Today, Ash Wednesday, we are all encouraged to enter a new chapter, a chapter that is itself brimming with possibilities and potential. God is calling us all into a journey of preparation for the great saving work of his Son. Today we begin the journey together, with an expectation of endless potential ahead of us.

**Creator God, just as you made the world with the possibility of change, so may you remake us during this Lenten season. May you awaken us to the possibility of change and growth as we let you into the darkest places within us.
Amen.**

Thursday after Ash Wednesday

*27 So God created mankind in his own image,
in the image of God he created them;
male and female he created them.
28 God blessed them and said to them, 'Be fruitful and increase in number; fill the earth and subdue it. Rule over the fish in the sea and the birds in the sky and over every living creature that moves on the ground.'
29 Then God said, 'I give you every seed-bearing plant on the face of the whole earth and every tree that has fruit with seed in it. They will be yours for food. 30 And to all the beasts of the earth and all the birds in the sky and all the creatures that move along the ground – everything that has the breath of life in it – I give every green plant for food.' And it was so.
31 God saw all that he had made, and it was very good. And there was evening, and there was morning – the sixth day.
Genesis 1:27-31*

I'm not sure there has ever been a "Top 10" list of Christian doctrines. A list of the best know Christian beliefs. However, if there was, I'm sure that the doctrine

Creation to New Creation

of original sin would be on it. There's nothing wrong with this, of course. It's central to Christianity. But perhaps it should be balanced out with another important biblical point? Original goodness.

In Genesis 1 God creates the world with the repeated refrain, 'And God saw that it was good', culminating in 'and it was very good.' God sees this world - the plants and animals, the sea and sky, the man and the woman - and he declares it all 'very good.' The very first word that is said about human beings is not how sinful and wicked they are, but that they are very good. Of course, sin soon enters the picture, and all of us fall short of what we could and should be. Nevertheless, the first thing God says is that we are very good.

This fact is actually central to repentance, and therefore central to Lent. The Hebrew word that is normally translated as 'repent' is the word *'tshuva'*. It literally means to 'return'. It's the moment where you realise you've lost your way. The moment where you wake up and see that you've gone wrong and you want to get back on track. The moment the light comes on. It's a positive, buoyant, zestful word - the moment of realisation. You are not an evil person who needs completely remaking, you are a good person who needs restoring. Like a window that is caked in dust and grime but that can be wiped clean.

> The first thing God says is that we are very good.

When I was a kid we used to find old 2p pieces that were all mucky and then soak them in vinegar to make them look shiny and new. The 2p was still worth 2p before we did it, but afterwards it was restored to its former glory. *'Tshuva'* is the moment of realisation that you need restoring. You fall short not of what you could never be, but of what you were made to be.

The New Testament Greek word for repentance is *'metanoia'*, which means 'wake up to what you're doing and change your mind'. It's the image of someone wondering off the path and then suddenly noticing and getting themselves back to where they should be.

Starting Lent in the story of God making the world and making his image bearing creatures (humans) may seem strange. Lent is about human fallenness. But repentance is actually based on human worth. You are fearfully and wonderfully made (Ps. 139:14). You are God's masterpiece (Eph 2:10). God knit you together in your mother's womb (Ps. 139:13). Repentance is grounded in these very facts.

So, as we journey through Lent and through the book of Genesis and explore many of the ways in which we fall short, we must never lose sight of the fact that the first word God says about you is that you are very good!

**Father God, thank you that you make us in your image and call us 'very good'. Forgive us for the times we leave the path and wake us up to how we have failed, so that we may be restored in you.
Amen.**

Friday after Ash Wednesday

> *7 Then the Lord God formed a man from the dust of the ground and breathed into his nostrils the breath of life, and the man became a living being.*
> Genesis 2:7

> *'Dust you are
> and to dust you will return.'*
> Genesis 3:19b

As I write this, there is poster hanging from my bookshelf just at my side. On the poster there is a hand full of dry dirt, so dry as to be almost dust. The dirt is falling through the fingers of the out stretched hand, like sand falling through an hour glass. Above the hand is written, in stark white writing, contrasting with the dusty brown of the blurred background, 'You are Holy.' I regularly look and ponder this poster, finding it helpful in two distinct ways.

In Genesis 3, humans are made through God breathing the breath of life into the dust. The word breath can also be translated spirit. So God breaths the spirit of life into humanity. In short, 'I am holy.' I, like you, am one of God's image bearing creatures. I am a carrier of the spirit of life. When I feel down, when I feel worthless or inconsequential, I look at the poster and remind myself that I am of infinite worth - worth so much that Jesus thought I was worth dying for.

However, there is another equally important truth - we are dust and to dust we shall return. We may be spiritual beings, but we are also natural ones. Made of the same decaying matter as everything else. We sometimes speak as though 'nature' is something outside of humanity, but the truth is we are also nature. We are made of the dust of the earth.

I find this truth helpful in two ways.

Firstly, when I fail it reminds me not to be too hard on myself. I am, after all, only dust. Reminding yourself that you are a fallen human doesn't always need to be a negative thing. If I was staying in a hotel with only a bed, lamp and single window, I would think myself hard done by. But if I was staying in a prison with the same facilities I may well think I was doing pretty well out of it. When you fail, remember you are but dust.

> I am dust, but I am also holy.

Secondly, when I feel I'm doing fantastically and my ego is threatening to get out of control, I also find it helpful to remind myself that I am just dust, falling through the fingers of time, like sand in an hour glass. Sometimes it is helpful to be put in my place.

Creation to New Creation

I am dust, but I am also holy. I am decaying matter and filled with the spirit of life. I am both worth everything to God and inconsequential to the infinity of creation.

I once heard a story of a Rabbi (I cannot remember where I heard it and may not even be remembering it correctly, but I find it helpful) who used to carry one piece of paper in his right pocket and another in his left. When he felt like his ego was getting too big he pulled out one piece of paper and read, 'You are dust and to dust you shall return' and when he felt worthless or desperate he took from the other pocket the paper saying 'You are fearfully and wonderfully made.'

This Lent, as we look at our sins and failings, let's hold on to both of these truths, for both are needed as we follow God.

Father God, in the times when we feel like we can do all things without you, remind us that we are dust and to dust we shall return and in times when we feel unimportant and mediocre, remind us that we are fearfully and wonderfully made.
Amen.

Saturday after Ash Wednesday

***2** By the seventh day God had finished the work he had been doing; so on the seventh day he rested from all his work. **3** Then God blessed the seventh day and made it holy, because on it he rested from all the work of creating that he had done.*
Genesis 2:2-3

I was recently told that the optimal number of breaths per minute for a human being is six. That's one breath every ten seconds. However, in pre-industrial countries the average number of breaths per minute is actually about twelve, whereas in the West the average number of breaths per minute is twenty. In the West we even rush our breathing! Busyness has become a pandemic in our modern world.

Many of us base our worth on what we can achieve. How 'successful' we are (which raises the question of what 'success' actually is). This results in a pandemic of busyness, with many sacrificing their relationships, families, health and mental wellbeing chasing after the self-worth that busyness promises but never delivers.

Creation to New Creation

Often subconsciously, we can base our worth on what we do.

My job brings me into contact with a huge range of people from all walks of life. Yet, in almost all contexts, one of the first questions is 'What do you do?' I am a vicar. She is a Doctor. He is a teacher. They are an electrician. The person over there is a chef. In todays world we are defined by what we do. If I ask you to picture someone who is long term unemployed, what image comes into your head? What if, instead, I ask you to picture a lawyer? Do you already have ideas of their worth? Their education levels? Their honesty? Whether we like it or not, we often judge people by what they do.

In a world in which we judge our worth on what we do, and often judge other people's worth by what they do (although we'd never dream of admitting either of those things,

> You are a human being, not a human doing.

even to ourselves), the fact that God stops for a rest may seem bizarre. After all, why would God need a rest?

Of course, as the bible continues, God taking a rest at the completion of creation is repeatedly used as the reason why we also should rest. We are repeatedly told to take a day off a week. A day to pause. We are also instructed to celebrate festivals - larger periods of taking time out. Maybe God takes a rest simply to demonstrate that he is not of ultimate worth because he creates the world, but because he simply *is* of ultimate worth?

In the same way, taking a rest, a Sabbath, is important for us because it reminds us, and indeed forces us, to remember that our worth is not based on what we do, but on who God made us to be.

You are a human being, not a human doing. Sabbath, forcing yourself to stop at least once a week, is vital to hold on to what really matters in the world. Sabbath - the day when we act as though all the work is done, even if it's not. Sabbath - the day to let our breathing slow back down to 6 a minute.

Lent is traditionally 40 days long, mirroring the 40 days Jesus spent in the desert at the beginning of his ministry and the 40 years the Israelites spent in the desert after coming out of Egypt. However, if you count the days from Ash Wednesday to Easter Day you will find it is longer than 40 days. Why? Because the Sundays don't count. Even our fasts and Christian devotions should have a rest. So tomorrow, and on each Sunday throughout Lent, there will be no reflection. Instead, lie in longer, walk slower, take deeper breaths and remember that even God took a rest.

God of the Sabbath, just as you rested on the seventh day, help us to resist the pulls of our culture, find time to rest and remember that our worth is in you. Remind us that we are human beings, not human doings.
Amen.

Creation to New Creation

Week 1 - Monday

7 Then the eyes of both of them were opened, and they realised that they were naked; so they sewed fig leaves together and made coverings for themselves.
8 Then the man and his wife heard the sound of the Lord God as he was walking in the garden in the cool of the day, and they hid from the Lord God among the trees of the garden. 9 But the Lord God called to the man, 'Where are you?'
10 He answered, 'I heard you in the garden, and I was afraid because I was naked; so I hid.'
11 And he said, 'Who told you that you were naked? Have you eaten from the tree from which I commanded you not to eat?'
12 The man said, 'The woman you put here with me – she gave me some fruit from the tree, and I ate it.'
13 Then the Lord God said to the woman, 'What is this you have done?'
The woman said, 'The snake deceived me, and I ate.'
Genesis 3:8-13

Often I fall into the trap of thinking about sin as breaking rules. Do not murder. Do not commit adultery. Do not lie.

Love your neighbour as yourself. Do not take the Lord's name in vain. Do not envy. I suspect most of us have kept some of them. While others we may struggle with. For example, you may be pleased to know that I have never murdered anyone. Yet, I'd rather you didn't ask me about envy. However, while all of these rules, and many more, are biblical, Genesis 3 actually points to the idea that sin is not primarily about breaking rules at all.

The first outcome of the fall is that Adam and Eve both realise that they're naked. Before this time they had been perfectly open with each other. There was no temptation to pretend that they were better than they were. A relationship of complete acceptance, openness and honesty. Then sin entered the world, they realised they were naked and grabbed some fig leaves. Their relationship suddenly needed filters. Human relationships have been filtered ever since.

This is why people's lives on social media often look perfect - which they're not. The perfectly-edited photos on social media are the 21st century's equivalent of fig leaves. Each of those times when you pretend you know what's going on because you don't want to look stupid or ignorant, you are putting on a fig leaf. Each time you present yourself in a certain way, or seek to create the right impression. In a million different ways, we have each sown fig leaves on.

But the relationship between people is not the only result of the fall shown in Genesis 3. The human pair are hiding from God himself. Again, we've been hiding from God ever since. Whether by convincing ourselves he doesn't exist, or that He won't mind about that behaviour, or

Creation to New Creation

insisting that he agrees with what we think is right. In a million different ways, we show that we are afraid of what God will do if he shows up.

The broken relationship between people and God and between people and other people is highlighted by the conversation God has with Adam and Eve. "The woman YOU put here with me - she gave me some fruit". Notice how Adam blames both the woman, and God himself for putting the woman there in the first place. In essence he is saying, "It's not my fault, it's the woman's fault. No, in fact it's your fault, you put her here!" I used to be a Primary School teacher, and I can tell you that the excuses are still the same!

The conversation also reveals one other broken relationship - "The serpent deceived me". The serpent, whatever else it might be, is also part of the creation. The relationship between humans and the creation is also damaged. You only have to look at our current environmental crisis.

> Repentance is not about obeying rules better, it's about restoring relationships.

I find that when I look at sin not as breaking rules, but as broken relationships with God, other people and the creation, I suddenly realise just how fallen I am. I know how much I want other people to think well of me. I know the hidden corners of my heart I try to hide from God. I know the times I take creation for granted.

Repentance is not about obeying rules better, it's about restoring relationships. Trying to be a better husband, wife, father, mother, daughter, son, friend or colleague.

It's about seeking to grow closer to God. It's about seeking to do my bit to restore this damaged world. Repentance is being honest about my failings, letting other people into the areas of my life I'd rather hide and endeavouring to make other people's lives a little bit better through my actions.

This Lent let us all seek to restore our broken relationships.

Father God, forgive us for our sins, the actions that we have taken that have hindered our relationships with you, others and the world around us. Help us to repent and find renewed relationship all around us.
Amen.

Creation to New Creation

Week 1 - Tuesday

14 So the Lord God said to the snake, 'Because you have done this,
'Cursed are you above all livestock
and all wild animals!
You will crawl on your belly
and you will eat dust
all the days of your life.
15 And I will put enmity
between you and the woman,
and between your offspring and hers;
he will crush your head,
and you will strike his heel.'
Genesis 3:14-15

21 The Lord God made garments of skin for Adam and his wife and clothed them.
Genesis 3:21

My daughter struggles to sleep, a situation made worst by her autism. A number of years ago we went through a particularly bad patch. Neither she, nor my wife, nor myself had had much sleep in days. I was stressed and tired. None of which excuses the fact that I lost my temper. I shouted. I screamed. I called my daughter selfish and uncaring of the rest of the family. I threw items across the room. At this point, my wife, quite rightly, intervened to try and calm the situation. I wish I could say I responded with calm. I didn't. Instead, I screamed at her too.

The worst bit was not in that moment, the worst part was later on as I sat on my own, tears in my eyes, deeply, deeply ashamed of how I had lost my temper and said horrible things to my family. I felt unable to look them in the eye. But worst still, I felt unable to face God. I was supposed to be a follower of Jesus, a person who turns the other cheek and returns love for hate. But I had failed, and I had failed big time. Finally I crawled back to my wife and daughter and apologised. They

> Forgiveness always costs.

forgave me. We hugged. The relationship was healed.

Somehow I found myself even more reluctant to face God. Like Adam and Eve hiding in the garden, I found myself metaphorically hiding from the creator. Eventually, of course, I returned and found exactly the same thing that Adam and Eve found, that God responds with forgiveness, love and grace.

One of the most tender details in Genesis 3 is that God clothes Adam and Eve. He could, of course, have destroyed the whole creation and started again. He could have insisted that he made them to be naked - completely open and honest with each other. But he doesn't do either of those things. Instead, he meets them where they are, and clothes them.

However, this grace and forgiveness is not cheap. Adam and Eve are clothed with animal skin. An animal had to die, the first death in the Bible, in order to cover their newly discovered nakedness. Maybe this is linked to the fact that forgiveness always costs. If you are ever in need of forgiveness, the bit of you that doesn't want to admit you did wrong has to die. And that hurts. Every time.

However, in the story God makes the garments. Adam and Eve's pain is taken by God and given to the animal. There's also the promise that the offspring of Eve will one day crush the head of the serpent, but not without the pain of the serpent striking his heal. A prophecy of Jesus himself. In Lent we are preparing ourselves for the cross. The place where all the pain and hurt of forgiveness and the fall will be endured and defeated. Each forgiveness involves a death, but God takes the initiative.

This Lent, look God in the face and accept his forgiveness. Not because you deserve it, but because he has already clothed you with his forgiveness.

Forgiving God, we are sorry for all the times we have hidden from you. Help us to come to you for forgiveness, not because we deserve it but because you are the God of forgiveness and restoration. You are the God of the cross.
Amen.

Week 1 - Wednesday

Now Abel kept flocks, and Cain worked the soil. 3 In the course of time Cain brought some of the fruits of the soil as an offering to the Lord. 4 But Abel also brought an offering – fat portions from some of the firstborn of his flock. The Lord looked with favour on Abel and his offering, 5 but on Cain and his offering he did not look with favour. So Cain was very angry, and his face was downcast.
6 Then the Lord said to Cain, 'Why are you angry? Why is your face downcast? 7 If you do what is right, will you not be accepted? But if you do not do what is right, sin is crouching at your door; it desires to have you, but you must rule over it.'
8 Now Cain said to his brother Abel, 'Let's go out to the field.' While they were in the field, Cain attacked his brother Abel and killed him.
Genesis 4:3b-8

After being expelled from the garden, Adam and Eve have children, Cain and Abel.
Abel grows up to keeps flock - looking after and breeding animals. Cain, on the other hand, works with crops -

growing food from the soil. We're then told that each of them presents a sacrifice with Abel offering the fat potions from the animals he farms and Cain offering fruit from his own work. We're not told why, but the Lord accepts Abels offering and rejects Cains. People have guessed why God accepts one and not the other but they are only guesses. The truth is, we simply don't know. Each of the brothers makes a sacrifice. One sacrifice is accepted. One is rejected. Cain reacts with anger and while God tries to talk to him and call him to a different response, Cain's anger explodes and he kills his brother.

The perfect world of Genesis 1 and 2 is now stained with murder.

We also make sacrifices. Young people voluntarily leave home and take on huge burdens of debt in order to get an education and a good job. Many people sacrifice energy and their own wellbeing for partners or children. Working adults sacrifice time with families and loved ones for their jobs. Sacrifices are all around us.

> You cannot control what happens to you, only how you respond.

Many of these sacrifices pay off. The university student gets the professional job. The loving parent produces loving and well rounded adult children. The working professional gets the promotion. However, some sacrifices do not pay off. Years invested in a marriage, but he runs off with another woman. Hard work in a job, only for the lazy person in the next office to get the promotion. Huge debt and effort getting a degree only to fail in getting the job.

The truth in life is that sometimes we make sacrifices and they don't pay off. The question is, do you respond with anger and bitterness, like Cain, or do we listen to the voice of God calling us down a different path.

The truth is you cannot control what happens to you. At some points in life things don't go our way, even if we did all the right things. The only freedom you have in these moments is in how you respond. With anger? Or with acceptance and gratitude for the gifts we have received? With jealousy? Or with best wishes towards others?

Because in these moments, just like with Cain, 'sin is crouching at our door', but we can choose whether or not to open that door. During Lent we acknowledge the times we gave in to bitterness and jealousy and resolve to choose the other path in the future.

**Holy Father, forgive us for the times when we have given in to anger or bitterness and help us instead to choose the way of acceptance and gratitude. When the sacrifices we make don't result in what we hoped, help us to resist the sin that crouches at our door.
Amen.**

Creation to New Creation

Week 1 - Thursday

11 Now the earth was corrupt in God's sight and was full of violence. 12 God saw how corrupt the earth had become, for all the people on earth had corrupted their ways. 13 So God said to Noah, 'I am going to put an end to all people, for the earth is filled with violence because of them. I am surely going to destroy both them and the earth.
Genesis 6:11-13

on that day all the springs of the great deep burst forth, and the floodgates of the heavens were opened. 12 And rain fell on the earth for forty days and forty nights.
Genesis 7:11b-12

Flood stories were common in the ancient world. Stories were told by the Sumerians, the Babylonians, the Mesopotamians and more. Stories about water coming and destroying whole communities and civilisations. There were also stories about people surviving these floods by building boats and stories about gods sending floods in anger to wipe the world clean and start over.

Creation to New Creation

All of this will sound very familiar to anyone who has read the story of 'Noah's Ark'. But while the similarities are striking, the differences are even more striking. For example, in the Mesopotamian flood story the gods decide to destroy the world because they are tired of human noise. Once the flood begins the gods go into a panic as they loose control of the water and have to flee themselves. After the waters calm, they are surprised to discover that (with the help of one of the minor gods) one human has survived. They discover this because they are hungry, as there are no longer humans around to offer them sacrifices. So when this remaining man offers a sacrifice they suddenly smell it and swarm to the location.

Compare this to the story in Genesis and the contrast between the two becomes obvious. The God of the bible destroys the world not because he's irritated with the noise but

> God is committed to living with people and respecting life.

because he's tired of the violence and corruption he sees. Throughout the flood, God is completely in control. Furthermore, it is God himself that instructs Noah to build an Ark, because he is a 'righteous man, blameless among the people of his time.' Most shockingly of all, the story finishes with God making a sacred promise, a covenant, that he would never destroy the world again. This God is very different - this God is committed to living with people and respecting life. A God who is after a relationship with people.

Lent is the time in which we face up to the violence and wickedness that is within us and make the brave decision to let God "flood" those parts of our hearts. But it's also, specifically, about letting THIS God do that. The God who promises never to destroy. The God who enters into covenant with people. The God of relationship.

It's also the time when we realise that we have let other things become gods in our own lives. Whether money, reputation or a million other things. These gods are hard task masters and often fickle with their affections. This Lent, let us commit ourselves to letting go of the old gods and instead surrendering ourselves to the God of Genesis. The God who is always in control, wishes to save us and promises to be the God of relationship. A kinder, more peaceful and more open God.

Loving Father God, we acknowledge that our hearts often hold violence and corruption. Please help us to surrender these part of ourselves to you and instead trust the God who is always in control and promises to be in relationship with us.
Amen.

Week 1 - Friday

But God remembered Noah and all the wild animals and the livestock that were with him in the ark, and he sent a wind over the earth, and the waters receded. 2 Now the springs of the deep and the floodgates of the heavens had been closed, and the rain had stopped falling from the sky. 3 The water receded steadily from the earth. At the end of the hundred and fifty days the water had gone down, 4 and on the seventeenth day of the seventh month the ark came to rest on the mountains of Ararat. 5 The waters continued to recede until the tenth month, and on the first day of the tenth month the tops of the mountains became visible.
Genesis 8:1-5

Certain moments can't help but stick in your mind, firmly imprinted in your memory, like a seal pressed in melted wax. As I prepared to leave the house, telling my daughters to get their shoes on, much as I had done so many times before, my phone vibrated as the screen informed me that my Dad was calling. While I found this unusual (I normally rang him, not the other way round), I breathlessly answered.

"Are you sat down?" He asked.

Creation to New Creation

"Yes," I lied.

"I've got cancer, I've been given up to 3 months to live." My life crashed around me. The next week was a blur, as so much of what I had always taken for granted evaporated in front of me. It turned out that 3 months was extremely optimistic, as only eight days after his phone call, my Dad died before my eyes.

Many of us will know the disorientation of our ordered lives suddenly disintegrating into chaos. Sometimes it is the loss of a loved one. For others it's the surprise of someone packing their bags and leaving without warning. Your business partner takes the money and runs. You suddenly realise that the alcohol or drug you thought you were in control of has you in its grip. So many of us, whether over night or over years, know the feeling of suddenly realising that our lives have descended into chaos.

> The God who can breathe His Spirit into the chaos of our lives and bring order and new possibilities.

The book of Genesis begins with the story of creation. "Now the earth was formless and empty, darkness was over the surface of the deep, and the Spirit of God was hovering over the waters." (Genesis 1:2). At first the world is chaos, formless and empty. But then the Spirit of God hovers over the waters, God speaks and order comes to the earth. (The word 'Spirit', in the Hebrew, is the same word as the word for 'wind', or 'breathe'. So the 'Spirit of God' could just as correctly be translated 'Wind of God'.)

Creation to New Creation

In the story of Noah, the order of creation is undone and the waters of chaos again cover the earth. Just as in many of our lives, it can suddenly feel like order has been lost and chaos has arrived. However, in the midsts of the chaos, God remembers Noah, he sends a wind (or Spirit) from God and order is slowly restored to the creation.

The God of Genesis is not just the God who created the universe, he is also the God who brings new creation, the God who can breathe His Spirit into the chaos of our lives and bring order and new possibilities.

This Lent, let's acknowledge those areas of our lives, big or small, that have descended into chaos and let's allow the wind of God to rush in and bring order and new creation into those depths.

God who brings order out of chaos, please breathe your Spirit into the chaotic parts of our lives so that we may experience your new creation and the renewal and possibilities that brings.
Amen.

Week 1 - Saturday

Noah was a righteous man, blameless among the people of his time, and he walked faithfully with God.
Genesis 6:9b

20 *Noah, a man of the soil, proceeded to plant a vineyard.* **21** *When he drank some of its wine, he became drunk and lay uncovered inside his tent.* **22** *Ham, the father of Canaan, saw his father naked and told his two brothers outside.* **23** *But Shem and Japheth took a garment and laid it across their shoulders; then they walked in backwards and covered their father's naked body. Their faces were turned the other way so that they would not see their father naked.*
Genesis 9:20-23

When we are first introduced to Noah, we are told that he 'was a righteous man, blameless among the people of his time'. This is an incredible statement. No one else in the book of Genesis is treated to the same praise. Not Abraham, Isaac, Jacob or Joseph. More than anyone else in the book, Noah is introduced to us as a holy, pure person. However, the final story of his life finds him drunk with his own children too embarrassed to look on him. How can someone so high, fall so low?

A surprising feature of Noah within the narrative is that he does not speak until right at the end of his life. God calls him to build an ark and Noah simply does it: 'Noah did everything just as God commanded him." (Genesis 6:22). God tells him to gather the animals and get on the ark and Noah does it: 'And Noah did all that the LORD commanded him.' (Genesis 7:5). Again and again we're told that the unspeaking Noah is given instructions and again and again Noah does what he's commanded.

When the water begins to recede you'd expect the, up until this point, fast paced story to quickly come to an end. Already by Genesis 8:5 we're told 'the tops of the mountains became visible' and yet Noah remains on the ark. Following this, Noah sends out a raven, who returns empty handed. A whole week later he sends out a dove. The next week he sends out another dove, who this time returns with an olive branch. Another week later he sends out a further dove, who this time does not return at all. Yet still, Noah remains on the ark. Not until God actually speaks, almost with frustration in his voice, and tells Noah 'Come out of the ark' (Genesis 8:16) does he finally leave.

> If God had simply wanted obedience he would have created automated robots, not human beings.

Often we can fall into the trap of thinking that obedience to God is the highest virtue, but if God had simply wanted obedience he would have created automated robots, not human beings.

Compare Noah with one of the other great heroes of Genesis, Abraham. In Genesis 18 God declares he is going to destroy the city of Sodom, but Abraham pleads for the city: 'Will not the Judge of all the earth do what is right?' (Genesis 18:25b). What does Noah say when God tells him that he is going to destroy the world?

Nothing!

Noah can't even get off the ark without instruction. You don't need permission to rebuild a broken world - get on with it! First and foremost, God doesn't want obedience, he wants your heart. We are called to love God with all our minds after all (Matthew 22:37).

Some things are obvious and we do not need to wait for instructions from God to do what needs to be done.

Noah did not need to wait for permission to begin the task of rebuilding the world. You do not need to wait for permission to begin the task of rebuilding the broken world we live in and you do not need permission to rebuild the broken parts of your own life.

So why did Noah end up drunk? Maybe it was survivor's guilt. Maybe he ended up this way because he realised he'd done nothing to save the world.

Noah, it would appear, ended up drunk and sad that he did nothing to save the world. This Lent, remember that if you simply concentrate on saving yourself, and no one else, then you may well find in the end that you haven't even saved yourself!

**God of both Noah and Abraham, remind us that you call us not to mindless obedience, but to love you with all our hearts, souls, minds and strength.
Amen.**

Week 2 - Monday

Now the whole world had one language and a common speech. 2 As people moved eastward, they found a plain in Shinar and settled there. 3 They said to each other, 'Come, let's make bricks and bake them thoroughly.' They used brick instead of stone, and bitumen for mortar. 4 Then they said, 'Come, let us build ourselves a city, with a tower that reaches to the heavens, so that we may make a name for ourselves; otherwise we will be scattered over the face of the whole earth.' 5 But the Lord came down to see the city and the tower the people were building. 6 The Lord said, 'If as one people speaking the same language they have begun to do this, then nothing they plan to do will be impossible for them. 7 Come, let us go down and confuse their language so they will not understand each other.' 8 So the Lord scattered them from there over all the earth, and they stopped building the city. 9 That is why it was called Babel – because there the Lord confused the language of the whole world. From there the Lord scattered them over the face of the whole earth.
Genesis 11:1-9

I was in an online meeting the other day and, while still listening, decided to move in order to make myself a coffee. What took me by surprise is that my computer camera followed me, zooming out and following me to the door! It turns out the technology now exists to follow a face around the room, meaning you can now move during an online meeting and the camera will follow you round. The older I get the more amazed I am at the huge technological leaps forward. In 1903 the Wright brothers flew a plane for the first time, by 2003 people were flying around the world in commercial airlines. When I was born the internet didn't exist, now social media can topple governments around the world.

Humans have the incredible ability to create technology that would have been unimaginable in the past. The last 200 years have seen technological advancement greater than at any other time in history.

The story of the Tower of Babel is a fascinating part of the book of Genesis. The people of the world speak one language and come together to build a city with a tower that reaches to the heavens so that they 'may make a name' for themselves. God then comes down to see and decides to scatter them over the earth because otherwise 'nothing they plan to do will be impossible for them.'

Central to the story is that the people 'used brick instead of stone and bitumen for mortar'.

We have a stone wall outside our church and when it needed repairing we needed to bring in a specialist, because building with stone is hard. Stones are irregular sizes and it takes time and skill to build with them. The height that you can build is limited. Bricks on the other hand are regular standard sizes that can be built to great heights, particularly once you use something for cement, like bitumen. In other words, the story of the tower of Babel represents a huge step forward in technology. The ancient equivalent of the computer revolution. Suddenly there is a whole new world of possibilities.

What is this new technology used for? Is it used to bless everyone? To build hospitals? To worship God? No, it's used to 'make a name for ourselves.' In other words, the people who had created the new technology decided to use it to elevate themselves and dominate those around them. Upon seeing this, God stoops down and scatters them so that they cannot continue. God sees how they are choosing to use this new technology and puts an end to it. It is not the technology itself that is the problem, but how they decided to use it.

> How is this technology used? For the betterment of the world, or for the elevation of certain people?

We live in a world where technology is everywhere. How is this technology used? For the betterment of the world, or for the elevation of certain people? Maybe during Lent, the even more important question might be, what is the role of technology in your life and how do you use it? Do you use your smartphone, or does your smartphone use you?

Let's give thanks for technology, but this Lent let us also remember that it is our duty to think carefully about how we use it.

**God who gives gifts of creativity and intelligence to people, we give you thanks for technology. Please forgive us for those times when we misuse it and give us wisdom as we consider the role of technology within our own lives.
Amen.**

Creation to New Creation

Week 2 - Tuesday

The Lord had said to Abram, "Go from your country, your people and your father's household to the land I will show you.
2 "I will make you into a great nation,
and I will bless you;
I will make your name great,
and you will be a blessing.
3 I will bless those who bless you,
and whoever curses you I will curse;
and all peoples on earth
will be blessed through you."
Genesis 12:1-3

"The arc of the moral universe is long but it bends towards justice." So spoke Martin Luther King Jr in 1967. With variations this quote has been repeated and reused regularly, being a favourite quote and vision of the former President of America, Barak Obama. The same underlying idea can be found baked into the hearts of many in today's world. Every time you hear someone say "You can't believe it in today's day and age", you are hearing the same sentiment - that history moves us forward. That we progress.

We used to believe that slavery was ok. Now we do not. We used to believe that women were inferior. Now we do not. We used to accept that certain classes of people were born to lead, while others were born to serve - "The rich man in his castle, the poor man at his gate, God made them high or lowly, and ordered their estate." - we don't accept that any more.

This is not the way the ancients understood history. Instead it was understood that history went in cycles. Just as the world went through its seasons of Summer, Autumn, Winter and Spring, so history went through its repeated cycles. History simply repeated itself. Your father farmed this bit of land, and his father before him. Eventually your son would do the same, and his son after him. The rich ruled, and would continue to do so. There were times of plenty and abundance, and then there were times of famine and desperation. Endlessly repeating and repeating.

> Can tomorrow be different from today?

It was in this world that Genesis 12 becomes so explosively radical. God calls to Abram and tells him to leave his home, his people, his family and do something different. God promises that he will create something new. God tells Abram that tomorrow is going to be different from today!

It is hard for us modern day people to understand the revolution that was taking place in this passage. Except, perhaps, that we are still stuck in those same cycles. Slavery still exists and many of us unthinkingly accept that that's just the way life is. Women often still aren't treated equally to men, but many of us simply shrug our shoulders in resignation. Rich Etonians still rule the country, while on housing estates families are still stuck in the cycles of poverty. Our economy still goes through the cycles of boom and bust. Can these cycles be broken? Can tomorrow be different from today?

If this is true for the world, it's also true for our own souls. Let's face it, so many of us are stuck in the same cycles of sin. What temptation do you regularly give in to? Have you given into it before? Deep down do you accept that you will give into it again? Is it possible to break out of the cycle? Is it possible that a new day can dawn and a new, freer, person can emerge?

Genesis 12 says that progress is real. That these cycles of poverty, sin and inequality can be broken. That a new world really can begin. That there really is a moral arc to the universe and God leads it to bend towards justice.

God of new beginnings, inspire in our hearts a desire to see the cycles of injustice within the world broken, and show us our part in the process. Stir in ourselves hope that the sins that have enslaved us can be broken and a new day can dawn.
Amen.

Week 2 - Wednesday

The Lord had said to Abram, "Go from your country, your people and your father's household to the land I will show you.
Genesis 12:1

St Augustine famously prayed, 'God make me pure - but not yet.' As a young man he lived in relative luxury and enjoyed what he himself would later describe as a life of sin. His Christian mother prayed desperately for God to intervene in his life. One day, sat in the garden, Augustine heard children singing 'Take up and read! Take up and read!'. He took this to be a sign from God to read the New Testament. Reading the book of Romans his life was transformed and through his intellect and scholarship the Christian world was changed. His book, 'Augustine's Confessions', is full of radical honesty and where we find the prayer - 'God make me pure - but not yet.'
The truth is that many of us, maybe especially during Lent, acknowledge our sins and desperately want to be free from them - but not today! Today we want the familiarity of our regular patterns and habits. Even if we know they may be wrong, we still find it easier to fall into

the familiar grooves of our bad habits than to make the effort of trying the new.

In Genesis 12 God speaks to Abram and calls him to a whole new season. God promises to bless Abram and turn him into a great nation. He promises to bless the whole world through Abram's family. He even promises to give Abram a land of his own. In other words God is going to fix the world that has broken and he's going to do it through Abram's family. But how do these promises begin? "Go from your country, your people and your father's household"! God instructs Abram to leave all that he is familiar with, everything he knows and understands, and instead go ... somewhere. Somewhere new and unfamiliar. Somewhere unknown and strange.

> We still find it easier to fall into the familiar grooves of our bad habits than to make the effort of trying the new.

What if Abram had stayed where he was? What if Abram had refused to leave? What if Abram's heart had prayed - "God do something new, but not yet!".

The whole of salvation history begins in Genesis 12. God's plan to redeem this world starts with God calling Abram to leave everything he knew. And, thankfully for us all, Abram agrees.

Does God want to do something new in your life? Maybe God wants to do something completely new and is calling you leave where you are and make that unknown journey. Maybe it's just that God wants to free you from the sin that has entrapped you for so long. You know that if you hang out with those people, that sin will happen again. Or if you have drinks and find yourself alone at night, that sin will repeat. It's so easy to fall into the same old familiar grooves that lead to the same old familiar sins.

But the God who called Abram is the God of resurrection and new creation, calling all of us away from our old lives of slavery to sin and into the freedom of hope and healing. Abram is called to leave behind the familiar and embrace the unknown. Is God calling us to do the same?

God who called Abram to leave all he knew in order to be a blessing to the world, give us the strength and courage to leave what we know in order to embrace the new beginning you have for us.
Amen.

Week 2 - Thursday

*3 I will bless those who bless you,
and whoever curses you I will curse;
and all peoples on earth
will be blessed through you."*
Genesis 12:3

Abram lived in the time of tribes. Everyone belonged to a tribe, and if you didn't belong to a tribe you soon died. Your tribe was your home, your family, your very identity. We live in an individualistic culture, where we largely work for our own good, and where the individual is the person of ultimate importance. Your rights. Your desires. Your hopes and dreams. But this was not the world of Abram. Instead everything was about the tribe. You worked not for your own well being and prosperity, but for the well being and prosperity of the tribe. Your possessions didn't belong to you, but to the tribe. As a tribe you fought battles, found food, negotiated with other tribes and took your part in the larger whole. If you did something good, it reflected on the tribe and if you did something shameful, that reflected on the whole tribe too. Everything was about the tribe.

Creation to New Creation

In Genesis 12 God calls Abram to be the father, or leader, of a new tribe. But then comes the surprise, because with this call also comes a promise, that through this new tribe God would bless "all peoples on earth".

It is hard for us to get just how shocking this is. The whole point of tribes was that they existed for their own blessing, and preservation. But God says that the tribe that Abram will lead is going to be different. This tribe is going to be for the good of all the other tribes. This was a whole new idea in human history.

So far in Genesis humanity has been on a downward spiral, but now God has chosen to start his work of salvation in the world and the way he chooses to do it is through humanity. Specifically, by blessing Abram and his family and calling them in turn to bless others.

> God gives you gifts not just for your own good, but for the good of the world!

This still remains the call of all followers of God. The truth is, that if you are reading this, you are blessed. The breath you just took is a gift. The fact that you can read this means you have had an education and can read. The clothes on your back, the food on your table, all of it is a gift. However, the radical message of Christianity is that these blessings are given to us so that we can bless others. God gives you gifts not just for your own good, but for the good of the world!

If we're honest, most of us do not naturally pass on these gifts to others but still act in the tribal identity of keeping them to our group - or even to ourselves alone. This Lent let's acknowledge the times we have done this and make the commitment to live as a blessing to the world.

God who blesses us so that we may be a blessing, forgive us for the times we have kept your gifts to ourselves, or forgotten they are gifts at all. Help us to live in a way that seeks to bless all those around us. Amen.

Week 2 - Friday

7 He also said to him, 'I am the Lord, who brought you out of Ur of the Chaldeans to give you this land to take possession of it.'
8 But Abram said, 'Sovereign Lord, how can I know that I shall gain possession of it?'
9 So the Lord said to him, 'Bring me a heifer, a goat and a ram, each three years old, along with a dove and a young pigeon.'
10 Abram brought all these to him, cut them in two and arranged the halves opposite each other; the birds, however, he did not cut in half. 11 Then birds of prey came down on the carcasses, but Abram drove them away.
12 As the sun was setting, Abram fell into a deep sleep, and a thick and dreadful darkness came over him ...
17 When the sun had set and darkness had fallen, a smoking brazier with a blazing torch appeared and passed between the pieces. 18 On that day the Lord made a covenant with Abram and said, 'To your descendants I give this land
Genesis 15:7-18

Have you ever wondered where the phrase, 'To cut a deal' comes from? The answer is this passage! Or, more specifically, the ritual that is described in this passage.

In Abram's day, there were no police, or legal courts. Instead, there were rituals designed to make sure that your word was your bond. The rituals bound the participants into a sacred, binding agreement.

So let's say that Abram wanted to make a deal with someone. At that time there was a ritual that sort to facilitate that process. Firstly, you would get some animals, maybe a cow or some birds, and then you'd chop them in half. You would then lay the animals out on the ground, with one half of the animal on one side and the other half on the other side creating a path down the middle of the animals. Once this was done, both parties would stand at one end of this bloody path and promise to keep their end of the deal before walking in between the animals saying something like 'If I don't keep my side of this covenant may I end up like these animals.' You had, quite literally, cut a deal!

> God does the work and calls us into nothing other than trust.

In Genesis 15 God tells Abram to get a heifer, a goat, a ram, a dove and a young pigeon. Abram immediately knows what is happening and so gets the animals and chops them all in half. Abram 'fell into a deep sleep, and a thick and dreadful darkness came over him.' Then God makes a promise and a 'blazing torch appeared and passed between the pieces.' In other words, God makes a sacred,

Creation to New Creation

binding, promise to Abram. A covenant. An unbreakable bond.

So far, so normal (at least for the time!). But what's strange? Abram did not make any promise to God. Abram didn't walk through the animals. God made promises, but not Abram. So what does God get out of the bargain? Nothing. Nothing at all!

When God makes a covenant, there's no exchange. God makes the promise which is not dependant on us keeping our end of the deal. This is true time and again through the Bible. Whether we're looking at the covenant with Noah, or the new covenant instituted by Jesus. God does the work and calls us into nothing other than trust.

Which brings us to the other strange thing in this passage. God enters a deal. This is a God who enters into promises with people. A God known by relationship. A God who gives himself, who binds himself, to people.

This Lent let's remember that God's promises of love, salvation and care are not dependant on us - God's promises are made without a requirement from us. This is the risk of grace. And let us remember that this God, the God who enters relationship with Abram, is the same God who enters into relationship with us.

**God of gracious relationship. Help us to trust in your promises, knowing that you give yourself freely to us. Help us to know that you are the God of relationship and to enter into that relationship with you.
Amen.**

Week 2 - Saturday

Now Sarai, Abram's wife, had borne him no children. But she had an Egyptian slave named Hagar; 2 so she said to Abram, 'The Lord has kept me from having children. Go, sleep with my slave; perhaps I can build a family through her.'
Abram agreed to what Sarai said. 3 So after Abram had been living in Canaan ten years, Sarai his wife took her Egyptian slave Hagar and gave her to her husband to be his wife. 4 He slept with Hagar, and she conceived. When she knew she was pregnant, she began to despise her mistress.
Genesis 16:1-4

In Genesis 12 Abram was promised that he would be made into 'a great nation'. In Genesis 15 he was told by God that he would have descendants. Therefore, it must have been frustrating for Abram and Sarai that they couldn't have children. To regularly feel like something has been promised, but to see no evidence of it ever coming true and the opportunity for it to come true slipping away, can be devastating.

Many of us may know people who grew up longing to be parents, only to find, as they grew older, that for various reasons they couldn't have children. But many of us may also have met the person who has worked hard for a company and yet always gets passed over for promotion. Then there are the ones who studied hard, got all the grades, completed the degrees, and still can't get the job they were always promised. The parents who invested in their children, only for the children to reject them in older life. The elderly couple who did the right thing and invested their savings for retirement, only for the economy to implode and their savings disappear over night. In so many ways, so many people, have felt deep in their bones that they were promised something only for that promise to fail to come true. Maybe that's true for you too. It's not hard to empathise with Abram and Sarai. They have done all the right things but not seen what they were promised come true.

> It's at the times where the promises are failing that we most need to throw ourselves on God.

In Genesis 16 Sarai comes up with a plan to force God's hand. In was a common practice in the ancient world for a slave to give birth on behalf of her mistress. While the birth was taking place the slave would literally sit between the legs of her mistress so that the child born would belong to her mistress. So a plan is hatched, a plan Abram agreed to, that Sarai's Egyptian slave, Hagar, will give birth and move the promise forward. Abram and Sarai think that they have figured out how to bring God's promises to fulfilment. Unfortunately, neither of them seems to have thought of checking with God! Soon the whole plan falls apart. Sarai is angry, Abram is useless and Hagar and the child are despised and run away.

When we feel like the promises in our own lives are failing to come true it can be very tempting to take the matter into our own hands. We all know the person who's been passed over for promotion who immediately starts telling everyone how useless the person who got the job is and how much better they could do it. Many of us might have met the degree holder who can't get a job who grows resentful and bitter.

However, it's at times where the promises are failing that we most need to throw ourselves on God. Pray for patience. Trust that the way of love and compassion is still the right way to be in the world. Follow God's call and trust him for the future.

This Lent let's acknowledge the times when not receiving what we feel we have been promised has driven us to act in ways God would not want for us. Instead let's commit ourselves to trusting in him for the future.

God of Hope. Be with us in the places where we have felt like our expectations have not come to pass. Forgive us for the times when we have decided to go down the route of dishonesty or resentment. Help us, this Lent, to trust you for the future.
Amen.

Creation to New Creation

Week 3 - Monday

5 Then Sarai said to Abram, "You are responsible for the wrong I am suffering. I put my slave in your arms, and now that she knows she is pregnant, she despises me. May the Lord judge between you and me."
6 'Your slave is in your hands,' Abram said. 'Do with her whatever you think best.' Then Sarai ill-treated Hagar; so she fled from her.
7 The angel of the Lord found Hagar near a spring in the desert; it was the spring that is beside the road to Shur.
8 And he said, 'Hagar, slave of Sarai, where have you come from, and where are you going?'
'I'm running away from my mistress Sarai,' she answered.
9 Then the angel of the Lord told her, 'Go back to your mistress and submit to her.' 10 The angel added, 'I will increase your descendants so much that they will be too numerous to count.'
Genesis 16:6-10

Genesis 16 presents us with an unusual and, if we're honest, somewhat shocking passage. So far in Genesis Abram and Sarai have been our heroes, the ones God has chosen to bring his healing to the world. God called, and

Abram answered. God promised, and Abram believed. Then we get to Genesis 16 and suddenly neither Abram or Sarai come across in a very good light. Firstly, they don't trust God's promises and decide to take things into their own hands. However, even more shocking is their treatment poor Hagar.

Hagar is a slave who, because her mistress cannot conceive, is told she must give birth for her mistress. Abram agrees to the plan and sleeps with the slave girl and she conceives. At this point we're told that Hagar 'began to despise her mistress'. Exactly what this means, or how this manifests itself is unclear. What is clear is that Sarai blames Abram for the whole thing! Sarai came up with the plan, but she blames Abram. Instead of pointing this out, or defending Hagar, Abram simply says Sarai can do whatever she likes to Hagar. Like many mistreated women before her, Hagar finally despairs and runs away.

Why is this story in the Bible? Clearly Abram and Sarai are the heroes of this part of the book of Genesis. We've been left in no doubt that God is on their side and going to bring his purposes about through them. Yet when we read this story there's no doubt that our sympathies, and the sympathy of the writer, is not with Abram and Sarai, but with Hagar. Furthermore, we're told that God himself sees Hagar, comes to her and blesses her. He 'sees her' (Genesis 16:13). Not just at a superficial level, but into her very heart. Hagar feels seen, feels blessed, and, on God's instructions, returns to her ill-treating mistress. Later on, in Genesis 21, when Hagar and Ishmael are sent away, not only does the writer again make sure our

Creation to New Creation

sympathies are with Hagar and Ishmael, but God also saves them and provides for their future.

Why put in a story that paints our heroes in such a bad light? Why put in a story in which God blesses and cares for a person who is clearly not part of the promised family and God's plan for the world?

One possibility is that we need to be reminded that, just because God is on our side, doesn't mean that we are perfect and doesn't mean that God is not on the side of the other as well.

The whole story of Genesis is about how God calls the family of Abram, blesses them and then promises to mend the world through them. And yet here we see that God also sees and blesses others. God sees and blesses Hagar. God sees and blesses the other.

> God may be on your side, but that doesn't mean he's not on the other side as well!

Of course, God's plan to fix the world only comes through the family of Abram. God only saves through Jesus. But does that mean he can't care for and seek to bless others?

What if God wants to bless Muslims? What if God wants to bless Russia (or whichever country we feel is acting wrongly at the current time)? What if God wants to bless the people on the other side of the political divide to you?

Maybe even harder is to consider that God wants to bless those Christians you don't like. If you are a traditionalist Christian, consider that God wants to bless the progressives. If you're a progressive Christian, consider that God wants to bless the traditionalists. Just imagine

that, even if you're right and God is wanting to work his promises through your tribe, God still wants to bless the other. The people who are 'holding the church back with their bigoted, backwards narrow-mindedness'. The people who are 'destroying the church through their liberal, anything-goes agenda'. What if God wants to bless the other? What if he sees them and cares?
God may be on your side, but that doesn't mean he's not on the other side as well!

God who sees us. Forgive us for the times when we fail to see others through your eyes, even the people we struggle with most. Help us to treat those we disagree with as people who are seen by and blessed by you. Amen.

Week 3 - Tuesday

5 No longer will you be called Abram; your name will be Abraham, for I have made you a father of many nations.
Genesis 17:5

In the book of Ruth a lady called Naomi goes to live in a new land with her husband and two sons. While there, her husband and sons die. Eventually she returns home and is greeted by the people that knew her before she left. But she tells them that her name is no longer Naomi, now they should call her Mara. Naomi means 'pleasant' whereas Mara means 'bitter'. Naomi declares that her core identity has changed. Who she is inside is no longer the pleasant person they knew. Instead the death of her husband and children has dramatically changed her very being. She is now bitter.

In the Bible names mean something. To know someones name was to know who they were. Names are about identity, about the core of someones being.

You'll see this throughout scripture. Later in Genesis 32 Jacob will wrestle with an angel (who may or may not be God) and is then renamed Israel, which means 'one who wrestles with God'. This is the name that the whole people of God go on to have. To be part of God's people is not to blindly accept God, but to wrestle with him.

In the New Testament, we see Jesus rename Simon as Peter, which means Rock. Jesus declares that Peter is the Rock on whom he will build his church. He gives Peter a task, a role, a vocation, a new core identity. He essentially says, 'From now on Peter, be the person who looks after my church.'

All this begins here, with God renaming Abram as Abraham. Throughout Genesis Abram has been promised that he will be the father of a nation. However, time goes on and no child emerges. Abram and Sarai even try to take matters into their own hands, by having Hagar give birth to Ishmael, only for God to declare that is not the way the promise is to be fulfilled. What we may miss through all of this is that Abram means 'exalted Father'. The one who can't have a child, in a culture in which names mean something, is called 'exalted Father'! What's even more surprising is that God renames Abram as Abraham - meaning 'Father of many'.

I wonder whether Abraham found this new name hard to live with. God isn't just changing the letters of Abram's passport - this is a declaration of who he is at the very core of his being. He may not feel like it. The evidence of his eyes may even tell a different story. But Abram is in fact Abraham - the 'Father of many'.

Who are you? In the very core of your being, who are you? Because we also have a habit of giving ourselves names. We label ourselves by our jobs - teacher, lorry driver, lawyer, shelf stacker, unemployed, retired. We define ourselves by our geography or ethnicity -

Northerner, Southerner, black, white, asian, immigrant, asylum seeker, city boy, small towner, rural. We label ourselves as left wing, right wing, liberal, nationalist. We allow our identities to be shaped by our mistakes or our past - addict, abuse surviver, abandoned child, widow, adulterer, school dropout. Illiterate. State school educated. Etonian. PHD. Hard worker. Outgoing. Introverted. Stylish. Listener. Compulsive. Autistic. Depressive. Lonely. HIV+. Anorexic. We even do it within Christianity itself - traditionalist, progressive, orthodox, evangelical, liberal, Catholic, Anglican, Methodist, Baptist, Pentecostal. So many labels that we use to define ourselves. So many names that we give ourselves. However, the Bible states something quite different. Because we're told that we also possess a new name, a new identity. We are 'a chosen people, a royal priesthood, a holy nation, a people belonging to God' (1 Peter 2:9). We are told to forget the old labels that we use to define ourselves, and instead embrace the new identity we have through Christ. As Paul puts it, 'You are all children of God through faith in Christ Jesus, for all of you who were baptised into Christ have clothed yourselves with Christ. There is neither Jew nor Greek, slave nor free, male nor female, for you are all one in Christ Jesus. If you belong to Christ, then you are Abraham's seed, and heirs according to the promise."

> We are told to forget the old labels that we use to define ourselves, and instead embrace the new identity we have through Christ.

(Galatians 3:26-28). Even more than that, as well as this group identity, each of us is also given a "new name" (Rev. 2:17). God has made you and just like he gave Abraham a new name for his new identity, so he gives you a new name. You have a task to do.

This Lent, throw off the old labels, and embrace the new name God has given you.

God who renamed Abraham, forgive us for the times we allow other names and labels to define our core identities and help us to embrace who you have made us and called us to be.
Amen.

Week 3 - Wednesday

The Lord appeared to Abraham near the great trees of Mamre while he was sitting at the entrance to his tent in the heat of the day. 2 Abraham looked up and saw three men standing nearby. When he saw them, he hurried from the entrance of his tent to meet them and bowed low to the ground.
3 He said, 'If I have found favour in your eyes, my lord, do not pass your servant by. 4 Let a little water be brought, and then you may all wash your feet and rest under this tree. 5 Let me get you something to eat, so you can be refreshed and then go on your way – now that you have come to your servant.'
'Very well,' they answered, 'do as you say.'
6 So Abraham hurried into the tent to Sarah. 'Quick,' he said, 'get three seahs of the finest flour and knead it and bake some bread.'
7 Then he ran to the herd and selected a choice, tender calf and gave it to a servant, who hurried to prepare it.
8 He then brought some curds and milk and the calf that had been prepared, and set these before them. While they ate, he stood near them under a tree.
Genesis 18:1-8

It is a well known trait within the Church that almost every regular member has a seat. I could easily tell you where each member of my congregation will sit when they come to church. You also don't have to go far to hear stories about the clashes that this has led to when a new person comes into church and dares to sit in someone else's seat!! I've even witnessed (although I'm pleased to say, not in any of the churches where I've been a member) newcomers being told to move because 'You're in my seat'. It's hard to imagine a less generous, more off putting, introduction to church.

It's worth remembering at this stage that Abraham lived in the time of tribes. You looked after your tribe, your people, your clan. It's in this culture in which Abraham is seated in his tent and sees three strangers walking past. Exactly who these strangers are is ambiguous. They could be three men, they could be angels, they could be God and two angels, they could even be the three persons of the trinity, but to Abraham they are three strangers.

Regardless, Abraham sees them and runs to them to welcome them (this is in a culture in which people, especially Patriarchs, did not run as it was thought of as undignified. It's also just after Abraham was circumcised!). He bows low to the ground and calls them Lord. He then offers to wash their feet and feed them. When they agree, he calls Sarah to prepare the finest flour - that's wheat flour, the expensive stuff. The stuff you save for anniversaries or Christmas (Well, they didn't have Christmas then - but you know what I mean!). He tells her to prepare three 'seahs' of flour. That's about 40 pints, or 20-25 litres. That's enough bread for three months! He then runs, again, to the herd, to sacrifice a 'choice, tender calf'. It's hard to communicate the outrageous generosity on display here. Abraham goes out of his way to give the most extravagant welcome to three strangers he's never met before and may never meet again.

But buried in the text is something even more shocking than that. The first verse tells us 'The LORD appeared to Abraham', then in verse 2 he sees the three strangers, then in verse 17 Abraham speaks to God about Sodom. Are these stories one story, two stories, or three stories?

So are we told that the LORD appeared to Abraham, then told how that happened? In other words, in the form of the three strangers, and then after the meal they talk about Sodom?

Or did the LORD appear to Abraham, then the three strangers arrive, then Abraham speaks to the LORD about Sodom - three separate events?

> To be a follower of God is to be generous.

In other words, did God appear to Abraham to speak to him, but Abraham interrupts God and asks him to wait while he attended to the three visitors?

This may seem shocking - but maybe Abraham placed the importance of hospitality so highly that he even asked God to wait while he cared for these strangers. Maybe Abraham had grasped the truth that serving God and showing generous hospitality are not two separate things, but the same thing.

To be a follower of God is to be generous. So maybe next time someone sits in your seat, you might want to let them

- and maybe even give them a smile and a welcome. After all, that's what Abraham would do.

God who calls us to outrageous generosity, forgive us for when we have failed to welcome and love the stranger. Help us to know that to serve you and to be generous to the stranger are part of the same call. Amen.

Week 3 - Thursday

> **18** *Abraham will surely become a great and powerful nation, and all nations on earth will be blessed through him.* **19** *For I have chosen him, so that he will direct his children and his household after him to keep the way of the Lord by doing what is right and just, so that the Lord will bring about for Abraham what he has promised him.'*
> *Genesis 18:18-19*

One of the greatest joys and biggest challenges of my life is that I am the father of two beautiful, funny, charming daughters. Seeing them grow is both the greatest pleasure I know and the greatest sadness. I love to see them discover themselves, embrace their passions and slowly become who they will one day be. But I also miss who they were. I miss the little girls who used to carry their toys with them wherever they went, who used to climb on my knee for a cuddle or hold my hand to cross the road. This is parenting - a gift some of us are lucky enough to receive.

The very first instruction given to humanity was to become parents - 'Be fruitful and increase in number' (Genesis 1:28). From the beginning God gave the gift of being parents to humanity. Anyone who can't be parent, for whatever reason, will tell you what a gift it is. However, what is perhaps less well known is that the Bible also tells us that this gift comes with responsibility.

When God decided to act in the world to save his fallen image baring creatures he called Abraham. Abraham is a hero of faith but is far from perfect. At numerous times through Genesis he makes mistakes and questionable choices. So why did God choose him? There is actually only one place in which we get the answer, and that is in Genesis 18:19 - 'I have chosen him so that he will direct his children and his household after him to keep the way of the Lord.' Abraham is chosen because God sees in him someone who will pass on his faith to his children.

> The most important place that the faith must be written is not on the page, but on the flesh of the human heart.

Later in Scripture, when God gives the law to Moses, he again emphasises the importance of passing on the faith to the next generation - 'These commandments that I give you today are to be upon your hearts. Impress them on your children. Talk about them when you sit at home and when you walk along the road, when you lie down and when you get up.' (Deut. 6:6-7).

The unique thing about the Christian faith is that we believe in a God who is first and foremost known to us, not through words and rituals, but through the flesh and blood person of Jesus. We believe in a God who became

human. Therefore, the most important place that the faith must be written is not on the page, but on the flesh of the human heart. There is nothing wrong (and indeed a lot right) with words and rituals, but the real place in which the faith is to be written is on the flesh of the human heart. When you realise this, you should realise that our number one responsibility is not to preserve church structures, or buildings. It's not to maintain systems or traditions. It's to inscribe the faith on the hearts of the next generation.
The truth is that I'm not sure I have been very good at that responsibility, and I'm not sure the church has either. Maybe this Lent it is time to remind ourselves that the gift of a next generation comes with the responsibility of doing everything we can to inscribe the faith on their hearts - as well as on our own.

Father God, thank you for the gift of parenthood. Whether we are parents or not, help us to take the responsibility of passing the faith on to the next generation seriously.
Amen.

Week 3 - Friday

15 With the coming of dawn, the angels urged Lot, saying, 'Hurry! Take your wife and your two daughters who are here, or you will be swept away when the city is punished.'
16 When he hesitated, the men grasped his hand and the hands of his wife and of his two daughters and led them safely out of the city, for the Lord was merciful to them.
17 As soon as they had brought them out, one of them said, 'Flee for your lives! Don't look back, and don't stop anywhere in the plain! Flee to the mountains or you will be swept away!' ...
26 But Lot's wife looked back, and she became a pillar of salt.
Genesis 19:15-17, 26

In Genesis 19 God destroys Sodom and Gomorrah because of their wickedness. We're told how two angels go into the city and Lot invites them into his house. However, the people of the city turn up at his door and demand that Lot send the two strangers out so that they can rape them. Lot offers his daughters instead!

Following this pretty awful display, the angels declare that they are going to destroy the city but warn Lot and his family.

Interestingly, despite every indication that Sodom is not the nicest place to live, Lot and his family seem very hesitant to leave. Eventually the angels have to physically grasp their hands and practically drag them out of the city. They are then told to run, and not look back. As they flee, Lot's wife looks back and is turned into a pillar of salt.

Why did Lot's wife look back? Why did Lot's family seem so reluctant to leave?

Sodom may have been a bad place but it was also their home. It was what they knew. Where their daughters had grown up. Their familiar house, the familiar streets, the familiar routines. All of it was in Sodom.

> You can't live in the past, and trying to will slowly turn you into nothing put a pillar of salt.

Change is never easy.

When I was 18 I went to university in Lancaster. While there I discovered my Christian faith in a whole new way. Firstly, I was was lucky enough to meet a group of Christians my own age, who became dear, dear friends of mine (with one of them eventually becoming my wife). I was also introduced to Charismatic worship. It was a time of huge growth in my faith, a stage in my relationship with Jesus that changed me forever. I give thanks for that time and for the friends and experiences I had. The lessons I learnt. The changes God made within me. I cannot deny that there are times when I long for that time. Days of excitement, little responsibility and seeing God move in exciting ways.

But life has changed. Life always changes. Change is inevitable, but never easy.

Some changes are good - like leaving Sodom, or a new job, or a new relationship. Some changes are bad - a loved one dies, a redundancy, a divorce. But all changes can be hard. Human beings like routines. We like to know what's happening and where we belong. Change can make us feel out of place, or disorientated. Change can lead us to look back with longing to what used to be.

We've all seen it - we've all done it. People who live in the past. When the kids were still small. When their husband was still alive. When church used to play those songs, we used to do this activity and we did worship this way. We all look back.

But you can't live in the past, and trying to will slowly turn you into nothing but a pillar of salt. If the world changes - which it will - we all have to look to the future, and embrace the new things God does. Otherwise we're just like Lot's wife, looking over our shoulder and longing for the past when God calls us to face the future and what he wants for us now.

This Lent let's make the decision to give thanks for the past but not live in it. Let decide, instead, to embrace the future. Whatever that may be.

Creation to New Creation

**God of new creation. We thank you for all the good things you have done in our past, but help us not to linger there. Help us instead to embrace the new things that you are doing. When you, like Lot before us, tell us to run for the hills, help us to run without looking back.
Amen.**

Week 3 - Saturday

10 *Now there was a famine in the land, and Abram went down to Egypt to live there for a while because the famine was severe.* **11** *As he was about to enter Egypt, he said to his wife Sarai, 'I know what a beautiful woman you are.* **12** *When the Egyptians see you, they will say, "This is his wife." Then they will kill me but will let you live.* **13** *Say you are my sister, so that I will be treated well for your sake and my life will be spared because of you.' ...* **17** *But the Lord inflicted serious diseases on Pharaoh and his household because of Abram's wife Sarai.* **18** *So Pharaoh summoned Abram. 'What have you done to me?' he said. 'Why didn't you tell me she was your wife?* **19** *Why did you say, "She is my sister," so that I took her to be my wife? Now then, here is your wife. Take her and go!'*
Genesis 12:10-13, 17-19

Now Abraham moved on from there into the region of the Negev and lived between Kadesh and Shur. For a while he stayed in Gerar, **2** *and there Abraham said of his wife Sarah, 'She is my sister.' Then Abimelek king of Gerar sent for Sarah and took her.*

> *3 But God came to Abimelek in a dream one night and said to him, 'You are as good as dead because of the woman you have taken; she is a married woman.' ...*
> *9 Then Abimelek called Abraham in and said, 'What have you done to us? How have I wronged you that you have brought such great guilt upon me and my kingdom? You have done things to me that should never be done.'*
> *Genesis 20:1-3, 9*

Abraham has come a long way in Genesis. Abram has separated from Lot, rescued Lot, entered into covenant with God, become the father of Ishmael, been circumcised, hosted angels and pleaded for Sodom. Time and again he's been taught the lesson to trust in God. He's been reassured by God that his promises are sure and certain. He's even had his name changed to reflect it.

But then comes Genesis 20.

In Genesis 12, right at the beginning of Abram's journey, Abram comes to Egypt and tells his wife Sarai to pretend to be his sister. He's so scared for his own skin, that he allows his wife to be taken into Pharaoh's palace. This leads to God's intervention, striking Pharaoh and his household down with disease. Once Pharaoh discovers the truth he is understandably cross, and sends Abram and Sarai away.

After all their journeying with God, in Genesis 20 Abraham again comes under a foreign kingdom and again tells his wife Sarah to pretend to be his sister. Again God intervenes and stops all the women in Abimelech's household having children until Abraham admits what he has done and prays for them.

How can someone who has come so far, immediately fall back into the same sin? Except, of course, that we all know that we do this. So many of us know exactly what it is like to fall into the same sins that we thought we'd left behind. We all know what it is like to give into fear, or peer pressure, or temptation. We all know what is like to repent from that failing, only to repeat it next time around.

I know people who have been trapped in the same sins for years, even decades. I've known people who have escaped addiction, sorted out their life, only to fall back into it decades later. I myself know what it is like to think that I have, by God's grace, left a sin behind me, only to discover it's come back.

Of course, when this happens, we need to repent and, through God's strength, seek forgiveness and a new start. However, it is also a comfort to know that, despite Abraham's

> It turns out, even though we go through the same cycles of sin again and again, God can still use us.

fall back into his old sin, God does not give up on him, or change His plan to work through him. It turns out, even though we go through the same cycles of sin again and again, even though it can sometimes seem like we just don't learn, God can still, and does still, use us.

Next time you fall into sin, do repent, but don't despair. God wasn't done with Abraham, and he's not done with you either.

Forgiving God, thank you that you are not only the God of the new start, but the God of the new starts. Thank you that when we seem slow to learn, you don't give up on us. We repent of those sins we keep repeating, help us to truly leave them behind, but help us also to trust that they do not disqualify us from your forgiveness and grace.
Amen.

Week 4 - Monday

*9 'Where is your wife Sarah?' they asked him.
'There, in the tent,' he said.
10 Then one of them said, 'I will surely return to you about this time next year, and Sarah your wife will have a son.'
Now Sarah was listening at the entrance to the tent, which was behind him. 11 Abraham and Sarah were already very old, and Sarah was past the age of childbearing. 12 So Sarah laughed to herself as she thought, 'After I am worn out and my lord is old, will I now have this pleasure?'
13 Then the Lord said to Abraham, 'Why did Sarah laugh and say, "Will I really have a child, now that I am old?" 14 Is anything too hard for the Lord? I will return to you at the appointed time next year, and Sarah will have a son.'
15 Sarah was afraid, so she lied and said, 'I did not laugh.'
But he said, 'Yes, you did laugh.'
Genesis 18:9-15*

> *2 Sarah became pregnant and bore a son to Abraham in his old age, at the very time God had promised him. 3 Abraham gave the name Isaac to the son Sarah bore him. 4 When his son Isaac was eight days old, Abraham circumcised him, as God commanded him. 5 Abraham was a hundred years old when his son Isaac was born to him. 6 Sarah said, 'God has brought me laughter, and everyone who hears about this will laugh with me.' 7 And she added, 'Who would have said to Abraham that Sarah would nurse children? Yet I have borne him a son in his old age.'*
> Genesis 21:2-7

Abraham's wife, Sarah, laughs twice in Genesis but they are two different types of laughter.

In Genesis 18 Sarah is past the age of child bearing, yet since Abraham and Sarah enter Genesis they have been promised that they would be parents, parents of a whole nation. Yet, despite the repeated promises, no child has arrived. They even tried to take the matter into their own hands, without success. It's understandable that Sarah begins to believe that, despite God's promises, she'll never be a mother. So when three strangers come and tell Abraham that in a years time she will give birth to a son her reaction is to laugh. Not a laugh of happiness, but a laugh of disbelief. Not an explosion of joy, but a snort of despair.

I was talking to someone recently who'd been going through a difficult situation. In fact, this was the most recent of a number of difficult situations that they had been through over years. As she was telling me, she laughed - "Sorry," she said, "I know it's not funny, but you've got to laugh or cry haven't you." Sometimes laughing is the only alternative to tears. Sometimes all the hope is gone and all you can do is laugh.

Despite Sarah's snort of despair, in Genesis 21 she gives birth to Isaac (the name Isaac means, 'He laughs'). Here we again find Sarah laughing, but this time it's a completely different kind of laughter. This is no snort of despair, this is an explosion of joy. In a world in which she thought all hope was gone, she unexpectedly finds a reason to hope again. After years of disappointment and failed promises, she find herself once again believing that promises can come true and the world can be better.

> God continues to promise that he can turn even the darkest of days into dawns of new hope.

It's easy to look around the world at the moment and despair. I don't think it's controversial to say that there's a lot wrong with the world today. Over the years I've worked in Wakefield I have watched as things for those on the bottom of the pile have got worst. More people are desperate for food. More people can't get the health care they need. More people are struggling to make ends meet. This doesn't even begin to touch on war, cultural division and climate change. If there was ever a time in which snorts of despair were understandable, maybe it is today - after all, you've got to laugh or cry. Yet God continues to promise that he has not given up on this world, and that his kingdom can break into our lives and our world. God continues to promise that he can turn even the darkest of days into dawns of new hope.

Sarah's snort of despair was turned into an explosion of joy. This Lent, when we find ourselves despairing and giving up on hope, let's remember that Sarah also gave up hope, yet found herself a year later in a place of joy.

May your laughter be not a snort of despair, but an explosion of joy - and if it's not, hold on because God may not be finished yet.

God of new hope, forgive us for when we give into despair and help turn our snorts into belly-laughs of joy. Remind us that you have not given up on this world and your promises always come true in the end. Amen.

Week 4 - Tuesday

Some time later God tested Abraham. He said to him, 'Abraham!'
'Here I am,' he replied.
2 Then God said, 'Take your son, your only son, whom you love – Isaac – and go to the region of Moriah. Sacrifice him there as a burnt offering on a mountain that I will show you.'
3 Early the next morning Abraham got up and loaded his donkey. He took with him two of his servants and his son Isaac. When he had cut enough wood for the burnt offering, he set out for the place God had told him about. 4 On the third day Abraham looked up and saw the place in the distance. 5 He said to his servants, 'Stay here with the donkey while I and the boy go over there. We will worship and then we will come back to you.'
6 Abraham took the wood for the burnt offering and placed it on his son Isaac, and he himself carried the fire and the knife. As the two of them went on together, 7 Isaac spoke up and said to his father Abraham, 'Father?'
'Yes, my son?' Abraham replied.
'The fire and wood are here,' Isaac said, 'but where is the lamb for the burnt offering?'

8 Abraham answered, 'God himself will provide the lamb for the burnt offering, my son.' And the two of them went on together.
9 When they reached the place God had told him about, Abraham built an altar there and arranged the wood on it. He bound his son Isaac and laid him on the altar, on top of the wood. 10 Then he reached out his hand and took the knife to slay his son. 11 But the angel of the Lord called out to him from heaven, 'Abraham! Abraham!'
'Here I am,' he replied.
12 'Do not lay a hand on the boy,' he said. 'Do not do anything to him. Now I know that you fear God, because you have not withheld from me your son, your only son.'
13 Abraham looked up and there in a thicket he saw a ram caught by its horns. He went over and took the ram and sacrificed it as a burnt offering instead of his son. ...
'I swear by myself, declares the Lord, that because you have done this and have not withheld your son, your only son, 17 I will surely bless you and make your descendants as numerous as the stars in the sky and as the sand on the seashore. Your descendants will take possession of the cities of their enemies
Genesis 22:1-13, 16-17

It's fair to say that there are some difficult stories in Genesis, but maybe this is the most difficult of all. What kind of God demands that you sacrifice your child? I don't know, but as a father I can tell you that it's the kind of God I want nothing to do with. As such, it's hardly surprising that this story is often cited by people who want to show how barbaric the God of the bible is. A God who demands you to be willing to kill your own child - is that who we follow? Do we even want to follow that kind of God?

Religion seems to have developed very early in human civilisation. From the earliest times our ancestors seemed to have realised that they were dependant upon forces they could not control. They needed plants to eat and survive, but if the sun shone too brightly the plants would die and if the sun didn't shine brightly enough, the plants would die. If it rained too much, their homes and crops would be flooded and destroyed, but if it didn't rain enough there was nothing to drink and nothing to eat. Disease could come and kill their livestock, or wild animals could eat them. In so many ways they realised that their survival was out of their hands and at the mercy of the forces around them. So early on they started to offer gifts to the forces to try and keep them on side. The forces took on names and attributes.

However, there was a problem in the system. If the crops didn't grow, or if the animals died, well then clearly the gifts they had given weren't good enough and they needed to offer more. But if the crops had grown and the tribe had flourished, well then it was clear you needed to show you were grateful, so you needed to offer more. So more and more was offered. More and more was needed and no-one ever knew when they had offered enough. Eventually, of course, people realised the only solution was to offer the most valuable thing of all - your own child.

This is why, when God calls Abraham to sacrifice Isaac he isn't shocked and he doesn't need to ask how. Abraham was an ancient human - he knew how this worked. So he gathered his servants and his son and for three days he travels to the place of sacrifice. For three days Isaac is as good as dead (that sound familiar?). Then Abraham tells his servants to wait while he and Isaac go to the mountain to worship. He then tells them that both he and Isaac will return!

Does Abraham know that something else is going on? When Isaac asks, he tells him God will provide the sacrifice. Is he lying to the servants and the child? Or has he come to know this God so well that he already realises that something else is going on?

When Abraham goes to sacrifice Isaac, God stops him. God then goes on to promise him blessings. For anyone hearing this story at that time, the shock is not that God demanded a child sacrifice. The

> Let's choose to believe that at the centre of everything is a God who is on our side.

shock is that God stopped a child sacrifice! What kind of God demands you sacrifice your child? NOT this one!

The whole point of the story is that this God is NOT like other god's. This is the God who provides the sacrifice. This is the God who blesses, instead of demanding more and more. Not to mention that this story points us to another son who was dead for three days before returning! (I know I shouldn't skip forward to Easter - but come on!)

The truth is that it's easy in todays world, just as in the ancient world, to succumb to the belief that the forces are against us and let anxiety dominate. Let's instead choose

Creation to New Creation

to believe that at the centre of everything is a God who is on our side, a God of blessing and a God who does not demand more and more, but chooses to give and to bless. This Lent, let's turn from the old gods, to this God.

God of blessing and generosity. Forgive us for the times when we surrender to the idea that at the centre of all things are forces that are against us. Help us instead to turn to the God who is on our side and chooses to bless. Thank you that while you would never demand our children, you still chose to give your son. Amen.

Week 4 - Wednesday

*Sarah lived to be a hundred and twenty-seven years old. 2 She died at Kiriath Arba (that is, Hebron) in the land of Canaan, and Abraham went to mourn for Sarah and to weep over her.
3 Then Abraham rose from beside his dead wife and spoke to the Hittites. He said, 4 'I am a foreigner and stranger among you. Sell me some property for a burial site here so that I can bury my dead.'
Genesis 23:1-4*

*Abraham was now very old, and the Lord had blessed him in every way. 2 He said to the senior servant in his household, the one in charge of all that he had, 'Put your hand under my thigh. 3 I want you to swear by the Lord, the God of heaven and the God of earth, that you will not get a wife for my son from the daughters of the Canaanites, among whom I am living, 4 but will go to my country and my own relatives and get a wife for my son Isaac.'
Genesis 24:1-4*

Genesis 16 sees Abraham and Sarah seek to take God's promises into their own hands by choosing to have a child through Sarah's servant girl, Hagar. While God acts graciously towards Hagar and her son Ishmael, He also makes clear that this is not how He intends the promises to come true. Trying to force God's hand to fulfil his promises is never a good idea. However, this truth also needs to be balanced with another, equally important truth. Since Genesis 12 Abraham has received regular promises from God. These promises basically break down into two halves, both of which are promised five times. Firstly, Abraham is promised the land of Canaan (12:7, 13:14-17, 15:7, 15:18-21, 17:7-8). Secondly, Abraham is promised a large quantity of descendants (12:2, 13:16, 15:5, 17:4-5, 22:17). However, by the beginning of Genesis 23 Abraham does not own any land, and has only one son (he also has Ishmael, but we are explicitly told he is not the barer of the promise). It is within this context that Genesis 23 and 24 have their significance.

Firstly, Abraham undergoes a lengthy haggling process in order to buy some land for Sarah's burial. While ancient Middle Eastern courtesy can disguise the fact, this proves a long and difficult bargain for Abraham. When you read, 'You are a mighty prince among us. Bury your dead in the choicest of our tombs. None of us will refuse you his tomb for burying your dead.', what lies under the polite conventions is the sentiment, 'You'll have to use one of our tombs, because we won't sell you one.' However, after a hard process, and at a hugely inflated rate, Abraham secures and buys one field and a cave. After decades of promise, Abraham owns some land. One field and one cave out of the whole land of Canaan. This is as much of the promise as Abraham sees fulfilled within his lifetime.

The next story tells of Abraham seeking to arrange a wife for his son Isaac. Just like the field, the bride price will cost him much wealth, yet he commissions a servant to take the money and find a wife for his son. Again the polite shows of generosity from Rebecca's father, Ephron, are part of the haggling process. However, the deal is made and Isaac has a wife.

The promises of God are often different from what we imagine. Trying to force God's hand is wrong, but thinking that God's promises will happen without human effort is also wrong. Instead God invites us to act in accordance with his will and promises help for us when we do. The outcome to both these stories is exactly

> God's promises act as our challenge and assurance as we work unceasingly to bring God's will to bear in the world.

what God said and promised, but they were only achieved through the total commitment of Abraham and his persistence in the face of difficulty.

God's promises do not mean that we can leave the future to God. Instead, God's promises act as our challenge and assurance as we work unceasingly to bring God's will to bear in the world. This Lent, listen to God's promises and call, and then take the brave step of doing your part to bring them into being.

God of faithfulness. Thank you that you are always faithful to your promises, but forgive us for the times we think this means we can be passive. Instead, motivate us to bring your kingdom to bear in the world.
Amen.

Week 4 - Thursday

***61** Then Rebekah and her attendants got ready and mounted the camels and went back with the man. So the servant took Rebekah and left.*
***62** Now Isaac had come from Beer Lahai Roi, for he was living in the Negev. **63** He went out to the field one evening to meditate, and as he looked up, he saw camels approaching. **64** Rebekah also looked up and saw Isaac. She got down from her camel **65** and asked the servant, 'Who is that man in the field coming to meet us?'*
'He is my master,' the servant answered. So she took her veil and covered herself.
***66** Then the servant told Isaac all he had done. **67** Isaac brought her into the tent of his mother Sarah, and he married Rebekah. So she became his wife, and he loved her; and Isaac was comforted after his mother's death.*
Genesis 24:61-67

There are days when I can't help but feel like life is simply a treadmill. Or maybe one of those travelators you get at an airport - those moving walkways that you step on at one end and it carries you slowly, but surely, to the other end. Sometimes it feels like life is simply doing the next thing that has to be done.

Get up. Work. Eat. Sleep. Repeat.

I've ministered to people who's whole lives have felt like that. I spoke to someone recently who told me with sadness that they had longed to go to college and university, but simply couldn't. They had passed their 11+ exam at only the age of 10. Fast forwarded early because of their intelligence. They went to the best school in the area and again did well. However, they came from a relatively poor family and their mother was poorly. As the eldest sibling, they had no choice but to stop at home, work and look after the younger siblings. They had no choice but to get on that travelator. It has been carrying them ever since.

> The truth is, even if you feel like you have no choices in your life, you can always choose faithfulness.

One of the fascinating attributes of Isaac in the book of Genesis is that he is almost completely passive. Abraham has been the main character since chapter 12 and will die in chapter 25. Isaac's children will be introduced at the end of chapter 25 and Jacob has taken over as the main character by chapter 27. Abraham makes decisions. God calls him and he leaves his home land. He rescues Lot. He makes a covenant with God. He father's Ishmael. He welcomes the three visitors and pleads for Sodom. In so many ways Abraham is active in his life.

Creation to New Creation

Likewise, as the story progresses, Jacob and his sons are active in their lives. Making decisions and following their own paths.

Isaac however is very different. His Father leads him up the hill to be sacrificed, and Isaac simply does what he is told. A servant goes and finds him a wife, and he meekly accepts the decision. He doesn't even get to bless the son he wants to bless (Chapter 27). Time and again things happen *to* Isaac. Isaac is the kind of person that life happens *to*.

However, there is always a choice. Isaac could have refused to follow his father up the mountain to the sacrifice. He could have rejected Rebekah. But in each case he accepted the situation and embraced it. Maybe it is this very acceptance that enables Isaac, despite his passivity, to be one of the heroes of the faith? Maybe it is his faithful acceptance of what God has ordained for him that allows him to be one of the legendary characters of the bible?

The truth is, even if you feel like you have no choices in your life, you can always choose faithfulness. If you choose faithfulness, like Isaac before you, you may find that God will still use you to bring about his plans and purposes in the world. Maybe Isaac felt powerless over his fate but God used him to change the world. Through faithfulness, may God use us in the same way.

Creation to New Creation

**God who holds the future in your hands. When we feel powerless over our lives, remind us that our lives are always in your hands. Help us to faithfully follow the path you set before us so that your kingdom may come and your will be done through us.
Amen.**

Week 4 - Friday

Now there was a famine in the land – besides the previous famine in Abraham's time – and Isaac went to Abimelek king of the Philistines in Gerar. ...
7 When the men of that place asked him about his wife, he said, 'She is my sister,' because he was afraid to say, 'She is my wife.' He thought, 'The men of this place might kill me on account of Rebekah, because she is beautiful.'
8 When Isaac had been there a long time, Abimelek king of the Philistines looked down from a window and saw Isaac caressing his wife Rebekah. 9 So Abimelek summoned Isaac and said, 'She is really your wife! Why did you say, "She is my sister"?'
Isaac answered him, 'Because I thought I might lose my life on account of her.'
10 Then Abimelek said, 'What is this you have done to us? One of the men might well have slept with your wife, and you would have brought guilt upon us.'
11 So Abimelek gave orders to all the people: 'Anyone who harms this man or his wife shall surely be put to death.'
Genesis 26:1, 7-11

One of my earliest memories is being in my Grandparents flat in London. I was sat on the floor watching cartoons on the TV. My Grandad walked into the room and said to me, "Watching cartoons, hey? I don't blame you. They're the only bloody decent thing on TV these days." I remember being shocked because an adult had sworn!

My Grandad was a fantastic man, but it's hard to deny that he could be very grumpy. When someone says the phrase, 'Grumpy Old Man' I picture my Grandad Gerrard. Another person I loved dearly, who could also be labelled as a 'Grumpy Old Man', was his son - my Dad. Even more shockingly, the older I get the more I feel like I'm slowly becoming a 'Grumpy Old Man' too!

It's an undeniable fact that these traits often get passed down families. Sins can also get passed down families. The child of an alcoholic is four times more likely to grow up to be an alcoholic. Someone who grows up surrounded by drugs is more likely to end up a drug user. Someone who's parents are driven by wealth and materialism is more likely to become materialistic. Jealousy. Greed. Pride. Violence. Judgementalism. Sins can pass down through families.

In Genesis 26 we come across a very familiar story. A story we have already seen repeated in Genesis. In Genesis 12 Abram visits Egypt and tells the locals Sarai is his sister. In Genesis 20 Abraham visits Abimelech, King of the Philistines, and tells the people Sarah is his sister.

Now in Genesis 26 Isaac visits the same Abimelech and repeats the same lie, that his wife is his sister. History, it seems, is repeating itself.

However, if we read a bit more deeply there is movement and progress going through this repeated pattern.

In Genesis 12, Pharaoh takes Sarai into his palace and, the texts infers, sleeps with her. This is then followed by Pharaoh and his household getting ill. Abram is sent away as soon as the truth is discovered.

In Genesis 20, Abimelech sends for Sarah, but before anything happens God appears to him and warns him not to sleep with her. The story ends with Abraham being sent away but him praying for Abimelech and his household.

In Genesis 26, Rebekah stays with Isaac and Abimelech discovers the truth by overseeing them in a passionate embrace. Isaac and Rebekah are then allowed to stay in the land, plant crops and are given Abimelech's protection.

The story repeats, but it also progresses. Each time the story is slightly better. Each time, with God's help and intervention, the sin is less severe.

> The truth is we can repeat the sins of the generations that have gone before us. But we can also do better.

The truth is we can repeat the sins of the generations that have gone before us. But we can also do better. We can make the same mistakes or we can break the chain. The truth is my Dad was nowhere near as grumpy as my Grandad, and (I hope) I am not as grumpy as my Dad. Children of alcoholics do not have to grow up to be alcoholics. The offspring of cruel parents do not have to be cruel. With God's help we can progress.

Creation to New Creation

History may repeat itself, but it can also progress. Why not do your part to help move the whole thing forward?

God of our ancestors. Forgive us for the times we repeat the mistakes of those who have come before us. Help us, through your grace at work within us, to break the chains of the past and embrace a new future. Amen.

Week 4 - Saturday

When Isaac was old and his eyes were so weak that he could no longer see, he called for his elder son Esau and said to him, 'My son.'
'Here I am,' he answered.
2 Isaac said, 'I am now an old man and don't know the day of my death. 3 Now then, get your equipment – your quiver and bow – and go out to the open country to hunt some wild game for me. 4 Prepare me the kind of tasty food I like and bring it to me to eat, so that I may give you my blessing before I die.'
5 Now Rebekah was listening as Isaac spoke to his son Esau. When Esau left for the open country to hunt game and bring it back, 6 Rebekah said to her son Jacob, 'Look, I overheard your father say to your brother Esau,
7 "Bring me some game and prepare me some tasty food to eat, so that I may give you my blessing in the presence of the Lord before I die." 8 Now, my son, listen carefully and do what I tell you: 9 go out to the flock and bring me two choice young goats, so that I can prepare some tasty food for your father, just the way he likes it. 10 Then take it to your father to eat, so that he may give you his blessing before he dies.' ...

18 He went to his father and said, 'My father.'
'Yes, my son,' he answered. 'Who is it?'
19 Jacob said to his father, 'I am Esau your firstborn. I have done as you told me. Please sit up and eat some of my game, so that you may give me your blessing.'
Genesis 27:1-10, 18-19

Genesis 27 is actually the second story about Jacob and Esau. We are first introduced to the two brothers in Genesis 25, where we discover that they are two very different people, with very different gifts.

Esau, we are told, was 'a skilful hunter, a man of the open country.' As you read the story you get the impression of a big, hairy, 'man's man'. Strong. Wild. Fun.

Jacob on the other hand was 'a quiet man, staying among the tents.' Mild. Meek. Delicate.

This difference is unlikely to be helped by their parents - 'Isaac, who had a taste for wild game, loved Esau, but Rebekah loved Jacob.'

At the end of Genesis 25 Esau comes home from the country hungry and finds his brother Jacob cooking a stew. As his brother asks for food, Jacob declares that he will give him some in exchange for Esau's birthright. The birthright was Esau's right as the older brother. Jacob, it seems, looks at his strong older brother and wishes that he could have what he had. Jacob dreams of being the older brother. Esau agrees to the deal and Jacob is given the birthright.

In Genesis 27, Isaac knows he is old and coming to the end of his life. He calls his oldest son, Esau, and promises to give him his blessing as the oldest son. Rebekah, on the other hand, has other ideas and conspires to get Jacob the blessing. This leads to Jacob dressing up as his brother, approaching his father and pretending to be Esau.

The truth is that we all know what it is like to look at other people and wish we had their gifts, their talents, their job, their life. We have all seen photos on social media of the carefully edited pictures of other people's lives and felt like we wished we could be them. Even in church. I have heard other vicars preach and wished I could do it like they do. Seen other people pray and wished I could lead like that. I know people who are cleverer than me, better looking than me. Have more money, better connections, more opportunities than me. I suspect I'm not the only person who has felt like this.

> God did not make a mistake when he made you *you*.

By now we are far enough into the book of Genesis to realise that it 'rhymes'. Certain stories, certain themes, repeat themselves. In Genesis 27 Jacob is asked his name and he replies, 'I am Esau.'

In Genesis 32 Jacob is again asked his name. He has spent the night wrestling with a man, a man who may be God himself. As the night comes to an end, the man asks Jacob his name. If this man is God, doesn't he already know Jacob's name? If so, why does he need to ask? Maybe the question isn't for God after all. Maybe God is giving Jacob another chance to declare who he is - Jacob. This time Jacob answers correctly, admitting who he is. God then immediately renames him 'Israel', which will become the name for the whole of God's people. It is almost as if God was waiting for Jacob to admit who he was, to accept who he was, so that he could finally use him in the way he wanted.

All of us have had the experience of wishing we could have someone else's gifts, but the truth is God made you *you* and God doesn't make mistakes.

God did not make a mistake when he made you *you*.

Once we have embraced the person God made us to be, with our own gifts and own talents and potential, then God can use us. Jacob needed to stop trying to be Esau, and start being Jacob, only then could God use him. God needs all of us to stop trying to be someone else, and embrace being ourselves, only then can God use us.

Creator God. Forgive us for the times we have bought into the lie that you somehow made a mistake when you made us who we are. Instead, help us to remember that we are fearfully and wonderfully made and you call each of us to your service.
Amen.

Creation to New Creation

Week 5 - Monday

35 *But he said, 'Your brother came deceitfully and took your blessing.'*
36 *Esau said, 'Isn't he rightly named Jacob? This is the second time he has taken advantage of me: he took my birthright, and now he's taken my blessing!' ...*
41 *Esau held a grudge against Jacob because of the blessing his father had given him. He said to himself, 'The days of mourning for my father are near; then I will kill my brother Jacob.'*
Genesis 27:35-36a, 41

I think it would be quite hard to describe Genesis as a story of happy families! Throughout Genesis we've seen families falling out, parents having favourites and family members banished from the tribe. Once again in Genesis 27 we see two brothers falling out, with one behaving deceitfully and the other declaring that he's planning on murdering his brother. The cycle of family hostility continues.

The cycle begins in Genesis 4, with Cain furious with his brother Abel and luring him into a field in order to murder him. Noah curses Canaan after his naked drunkenness

Creation to New Creation

(Genesis 9). Abraham and Lot have to go separate ways after their two families are incapable of staying together without quarrelling (Genesis 13). Ishmael, half-brother of Isaac, is sent away with his mother Hagar (Genesis 21). After the break down in relationship between Jacob and Esau the cycle continues, as Jacob's son, Joseph, will be sold by his brothers into slavery in Egypt (Genesis 37). Time and again in Genesis, families are divided and hostile to each other.

Is history doomed to repeat itself? Are we doomed to repeat our sins, over and over and over again? Can we ever progress? Is it possible for tomorrow to be different from today?

> Genesis may present us with a repeating pattern of family breakdown, but it also shows progress, reunion and reconciliation.

Yet hidden just below the surface of the story, there is something else going on.

The first broken relationship is between Cain and Abel. A relationship that results in murder. Which, inevitably, means a permanent breaking of relationship.

Noah curses Canaan, but both parties are still alive and so the possibility of healing and forgiveness is still there - even if it never takes place.

Abraham and Lot go their separate ways, but Abraham still rescues Lot in Genesis 14. While there's no sign of them ever talking, and reconciling, Abraham still shows family loyalty to his nephew.

Ishmael, along with his mother Hagar, are sent away. However, when Abraham dies we are told that Isaac and Ishmael bury him together - '[Abraham's] sons Isaac and Ishmael buried him in the cave.' (Genesis 25:9). While their relationship has no indication of closeness, there must have been some reconciliation between them, even if it was only an agreement to bury their dad together.

In our current story, Esau declares he will kill his brother Jacob. However, by the end of the story we will see a touching reunion between them, with reconciliation and the restoration of their relationship - 'Esau ran to meet Jacob and embraced him; he threw his arms around his neck and kissed him.' (Genesis 33:4). Jacob and Esau still go their separate ways, but at peace with each other.

Finally, Joseph will be sold into slavery by his brothers, but there also will be reconciliation and restoration. This time the brothers will even come to live with him in Egypt.

Genesis may present us with a repeating pattern of family breakdown, but it also shows progress, reunion and reconciliation.

We may repeat the same sins, but that does not mean that we can not make headway in the right direction. Tomorrow does not have to be the same as today. Never believe the lie that you are stuck where you are. You can move forward, even if it is an inch at a time.

**God of Abraham, Isaac and Jacob, please forgive us for the times when we buy into the lie that we are stuck in the same repeated patterns. Help us to trust that, with you and in your strength, progress can and will be made.
Amen.**

Week 5 - Tuesday

***42** When Rebekah was told what her elder son Esau had said, she sent for her younger son Jacob and said to him, 'Your brother Esau is planning to avenge himself by killing you. **43** Now then, my son, do what I say: flee at once to my brother Laban in Harran. **44** Stay with him for a while until your brother's fury subsides.*
Genesis 27:42-44

Today we encounter yet another repeating theme in the book of Genesis, the story of someone having to leave their home. Jacob has cheated his brother out of his birthright and out of his father's blessing and, as a result, Esau wants to kill him. Jacob has no choice but to leave everything he has ever known - his family, his life, all his relationships - and head out into the unknown.

Genesis begins with the story of exile - Adam and Eve thrown out of the garden into the unknown. Humanity in exile. Humanity loosing their home, their refuge, their security.

Later God calls Abraham and tells him to leave his home and go where God leads him. So Abraham heads out into the unknown.

Creation to New Creation

By the end of the book of Genesis the whole of Abraham's family will again leave their home and find themselves exiled in Egypt. The promise of a home in the land of Canaan a seemingly impossible dream.

Home is where things "fit" you. You know where things are. You know where the pans are, where your t-shirt draw is, where the salt is kept. You know how to work the shower and how to turn on the TV. The food in the fridge is the food you and your loved ones like. The things on the shelves reflect your interests and your desires. Home is where things "fit" you.

To be in exile is to be in the place where things don't fit. The language, the food, the music. All of it seems alien. You feel out of place and uncertain.

> God is with us in the exile and will use it for His purposes.

Of course, while there are thousands of refugees and alyssum seekers in the world, most of us are lucky enough to not experience physical exile first hand. But all of us, at some point or another, have experienced spiritual exile. Your partner leaves you for someone else. You loose your job. A loved one dies. Suddenly things don't make sense. The future no longer seems secure. What we thought was permanent and certain has proved temporary and unstable. Ultimately, all humanity feels in exile. We live in a world with illness, disease, war and death and yet our very souls cry out against them. We are in exile. These things don't "fit" humanity.

Creation to New Creation

Jacob lived in a world in which people understood there to be different god's in different places. As Jacob leaves his family and all he has known, he may well have thought he was leaving his God behind too. However, Jacob was to discover that this God went with him. That the God of his fathers, Abraham and Isaac, was the God who went with him into exile. In fact, Jacob will leave his home as Jacob, but return as Israel. It is actually in exile that God is most with him and most transforms him into the person he calls him to be.

This is true for Abraham and the whole of Jacob's family in Egypt. God is with them in the exile and actually uses the time of exile to transform them into his people.

The writer of Genesis is making the point that what is true of Abraham and Jacob, will also be true of Adam, Eve and the whole of humanity. God is with us in the exile and will use it for His purposes.

This is ultimately shown in Jesus himself. The Jesus who goes into the wilderness after his baptism. The Jesus who is betrayed by Judas. The Jesus who is abandoned by his friends. The Jesus who goes to the cross. Jesus - God himself in the worst of exiles.

Lent itself is actually to take on a voluntary exile. To make a journey into the wilderness. To leave behind something of home, in the certainty that God will meet us in the wilderness.

So next time you feel like you're in exile, don't despair. Remember that God is with you even in this, and, if you let him, he will use even this.

God of exile. Just as you were with Abraham and Jacob in their exiles, help us to remember that you are with us in our exiles. When we feel like all that we know has disappeared and we do not know where to turn, remind us that you are still with us.
Amen.

Week 5 - Wednesday

10 *Jacob left Beersheba and set out for Harran.* **11** *When he reached a certain place, he stopped for the night because the sun had set. Taking one of the stones there, he put it under his head and lay down to sleep.* **12** *He had a dream in which he saw a stairway resting on the earth, with its top reaching to heaven, and the angels of God were ascending and descending on it.* **13** *There above it stood the Lord, and he said: 'I am the Lord, the God of your father Abraham and the God of Isaac. I will give you and your descendants the land on which you are lying.* **14** *Your descendants will be like the dust of the earth, and you will spread out to the west and to the east, to the north and to the south. All peoples on earth will be blessed through you and your offspring.* **15** *I am with you and will watch over you wherever you go, and I will bring you back to this land. I will not leave you until I have done what I have promised you.'*
16 *When Jacob awoke from his sleep, he thought, 'Surely the Lord is in this place, and I was not aware of it.'*
Genesis 28:10-16

Jacob enters the wilderness, probably assuming that he was leaving God behind him. Imagine him setting out for Harran, walking through the wilderness, replaying the events of his life that have led to this place. Questioning the decisions that led to him having to flee home for fear of his life. Wondering whether he ever should have asked for Esau's birthright. Replaying whether he should have stood up to his mother when she suggested he take Esau's place to get his father's blessing. Trying to picture what the future would be like. Would his uncle, who he's probably never met, welcome him? Does he even have a future?

Eventually, probably exhausted, he settles down to sleep for the night, using nothing but a stone for a pillow. As he sleeps he has a dream in which he sees angels ascending and descending on a stairway and at the top the Lord himself. As Jacob awakes he says,

> Jacob realises that God was already there, it's just he was too wrapped up in his own worries and concerns to notice.

'Surely the Lord is in this place, and I was not aware of it'!!

This line is incredible. It's easy to skip over it and not notice the implications. Jacob does not say, 'God wasn't here, but now he's turned up'. Instead, Jacob realises that God was already there, it's just he was too wrapped up in his own worries and concerns to notice. The Lord of all creation, the one who created the stars and sustains this world, was with Jacob as he walked into the wilderness, but he was too distracted to see it.

This is a message repeated throughout the bible - the whole world is saturated in God and transcendence. The earth is drenched with God, suffused with his glory, engulfed with his presence. "Where can I go from your Spirit? Where can I flee from your presence?", as it says in Psalm 139.

Too often I've heard Christians say things like, 'And then God turned up'. But where do you think he was before that? It's not God who turns up, it is us who wake up. Like Jacob awaking from his dream, we suddenly become alert to the fact that was always true - God is here.

The truth is I sympathise with Jacob. I too sometimes get caught up in my own thoughts and fail to notice that God is already here. I too sometimes find myself saying, 'Surely God was in this place, and I was not aware of it.'

Maybe, like me, you, in times of difficulty and stress, would benefit from stopping long enough to notice the presence of God all around you. This Lent, let's commit to waking up to the transcendent presence of God all around us.

God in whom we live and breathe and have our being. Forgive us for the times where we are too busy to notice you. Help us to see your presence and your glory all around us.
Amen.

Creation to New Creation

Week 5 - Thursday

*16 Now Laban had two daughters; the name of the elder one was Leah, and the name of the younger was Rachel. 17 Leah had weak eyes, but Rachel had a lovely figure and was beautiful. 18 Jacob was in love with Rachel and said, 'I'll work for you seven years in return for your younger daughter Rachel.' ...
22 So Laban brought together all the people of the place and gave a feast. 23 But when evening came, he took his daughter Leah and brought her to Jacob, and Jacob made love to her. 24 And Laban gave his servant Zilpah to his daughter as her attendant.
25 When morning came, there was Leah! So Jacob said to Laban, 'What is this you have done to me? I served you for Rachel, didn't I? Why have you deceived me?'
26 Laban replied, 'It is not our custom here to give the younger daughter in marriage before the elder one. 27 Finish this daughter's bridal week; then we will give you the younger one also, in return for another seven years of work.'
28 And Jacob did so. He finished the week with Leah, and then Laban gave him his daughter Rachel to be his wife. 29 Laban gave his servant Bilhah to his daughter Rachel*

*as her attendant. **30** Jacob made love to Rachel also, and his love for Rachel was greater than his love for Leah. And he worked for Laban another seven years.*
Genesis 29:16-18, 22-30

It's easy to forget the the Bible was not designed to be read, but to be heard. The first recipients of Genesis would not have read it, but would have heard it read out loud to them. Hearing something is a different experience to reading something. It is possible to take in a whole sentence at once when you read, but it is not possible to know the end of a sentence before you've heard it. This is why jokes always work better out loud. As such, Genesis, and the rest of scripture, often uses sentence structures that work best when read out loud.
In Genesis 29 Jacob has fled from his brother Esau and travelled to the house of his uncle Laban. Once there he meets Rachel, Laban's daughter, and falls dramatically in love. So a deal is struck - Jacob will work for Laban for seven years in return for Rachel's hand in marriage. Once the seven years have passed, the joyous wedding takes place. However, Jacob wakes up in the morning to discover that Laban has swapped Rachel for her older sister, Leah. Jacob is understandably angry, but Laban insists that it's not right for the youngest sister to marry before the eldest. In return for another 7 years work Laban agrees to let Jacob marry Rachel. Luckily, Jacob does not have to wait until the end of the seven years, but instead can marries Rachel a week later. We are then told: 'Jacob made love to Rachel also, and his love for Rachel was greater than his love for Leah.'

The Hebrew actually structures this sentence slightly differently, so that the end of the sentence subverts the hearers expectations. Perhaps an alternative translation would be:

'Jacob *also* married Rachel, and he *also* loved Rachel ...'

The use of the word '*also*' for the hearer has clear implications. It suggests that Jacob loves both Leah and Rachel equally. It seems we have a happy ending. The long theme of sibling rivalry in Genesis is reaching its climax as Jacob embraces both sisters equally. But then the sentence brings all this crashing down:

'... more than Leah.'

The second *also* doesn't actually make sense. You can love Rachel and also Leah. You can love Rachel more than Leah. You can't do both. The sentence is written so that the end takes you by surprise.

> The God of Genesis is the God who sees those who are unseen by everyone else.

When we are introduced to Leah in Genesis 29:16-17 we are told that Leah 'had weak eyes.' There are a number of possible meanings to this verse. It could be a way of saying that Leah was unattractive. It could mean that her eyes were very sensitive, and she was unable to go out in the sun. However, it could also mean that she is easily moved to tears. That Leah was a person who felt things very deeply. If this is the case, Leah is now set on a life in which she knows that she is the lesser love of her husband. Even the names she gives her children suggest that she is pleading for her husband's affection and attention (Genesis 29:32-35).

It is with this in mind that we should notice that Jesus comes from the line of Leah, the line of Judah. The God of Genesis is the God of the unloved, the unnoticed, the uncared for. The God of Genesis is the God who sees those who are unseen by everyone else.

This Lent, let's commit to seeing those who other people do not see. The refugee, the homeless, the isolated pensioner. Let's notice those that God notices.

And if you feel unnoticed, or unloved, take comfort in the knowledge that God is biased in your direction. He notices, he loves, he cares.

God of the unloved. Help us to see people through your eyes and help us always to notice those people others ignore. When we feel unloved, help us to remember that you are the God who is biased in favour of those other people fail to notice.
Amen.

Week 5 - Friday

24 So Jacob was left alone, and a man wrestled with him till daybreak. 25 When the man saw that he could not overpower him, he touched the socket of Jacob's hip so that his hip was wrenched as he wrestled with the man. 26 Then the man said, 'Let me go, for it is daybreak.' But Jacob replied, 'I will not let you go unless you bless me.'
27 The man asked him, 'What is your name?'
'Jacob,' he answered.
28 Then the man said, 'Your name will no longer be Jacob, but Israel, because you have struggled with God and with humans and have overcome.'
Genesis 32:24-28

As Jacob leaves Laban's house, ultimately to be reconciled to his brother Esau, he sends the rest of his family ahead of him. For the second time in his life he finds himself alone in the wilderness. The first time this happened he was fleeing for his life, uncertain what the future held. In the wilderness he dreamed of a staircase to heaven and awoke to declare 'Surely God was in this place and I was not aware of it.' Years later he makes the same journey in reverse. He is again fleeing his family (this time his uncle and father-in-law Laban and his sons) and is again heading into the unknown. Would his brother welcome him? Would he still be angry and determined to kill him? After many years of hard work, Jacob must have felt like he was back where he started.

Then, out in the wilderness, we are told that a man comes and wrestles with him. Throughout the night they struggle and grapple together. While neither could overcome the other, the mysterious man does wrench Jacob's hip from its socket. But still Jacob refuses to let go. Finally the man asks Jacob's name, before renaming him - 'Your name will no longer be Jacob, but Israel, because you have struggled with God and with humans and have overcome.' From this point on Jacob's name is Israel, the name that will be given to the whole people of God.

> God wants people that do not let him off the hook!

Why, out of all the names God could have given Jacob and his people, why does he choose Israel? Israel means 'he who struggles with God.'

Sometimes the Christian community can fall into the trap of believing that, because to be a Christian is to have faith, then questions are not allowed. The world is full of pain and suffering. Sometimes we, like Jacob, work for years only to suddenly feel like we're back where we started. Sometimes someone we love gets ill, or it feels like the things we have put our faith in have failed us. When that happens, what is the Christian response? Do we simply

accept it is the will of God, pretending that it doesn't hurt? Or do we wrestle with God? Do we demand he answer us? Already in Genesis we have seen Abraham question God. If we continue in the scriptures we will encounter the raw, emotional anger of the Psalms:
'How long, LORD? Will you forget me for ever?
How long must I wrestle with my thoughts
and day after day have sorrow in my heart?
How long will my enemy triumph over me?
Look on me and answer, LORD my God.' (Psalm 13:1-3a)
To be a Christian is to live with the tension of what we live with, in the exile of life, and what we hope for in God. It's to live in the now and the not yet. To know that the world is fallen, but also to know that the tomb in empty. Wrestling with God is the expression of that.
Why did God call his people Israel? Because to be a follower of this God is to be a wrestler with God until he fulfils his promise. God wants people that do not let him off the hook!

God of those who wrestle. Give us the courage to hold you to account when we see the fallen world around us. Thank you that you do not call blind servants, but thinking and passionate co-workers. Help us to be those who wrestle with you, the world and ourselves. Amen.

Week 5 - Saturday

Now Dinah, the daughter Leah had borne to Jacob, went out to visit the women of the land. **2** *When Shechem son of Hamor the Hivite, the ruler of that area, saw her, he took her and raped her.* **3** *His heart was drawn to Dinah daughter of Jacob; he loved the young woman and spoke tenderly to her.* **4** *And Shechem said to his father Hamor, 'Get me this girl as my wife.' ...*
Hamor said to them, 'My son Shechem has his heart set on your daughter. Please give her to him as his wife. **9** *Intermarry with us; give us your daughters and take our daughters for yourselves.* **10** *You can settle among us; the land is open to you. Live in it, trade in it, and acquire property in it.' ...*
14 *They said to them, 'We can't do such a thing; we can't give our sister to a man who is not circumcised. That would be a disgrace to us.* **15** *We will enter into an agreement with you on one condition only: that you become like us by circumcising all your males. ...*
24 *All the men who went out of the city gate agreed with Hamor and his son Shechem, and every male in the city was circumcised.*

Creation to New Creation

25 Three days later, while all of them were still in pain, two of Jacob's sons, Simeon and Levi, Dinah's brothers, took their swords and attacked the unsuspecting city, killing every male.
Genesis 34:1-4, 8-10, 14-15, 24-25

It's hard not to be shocked by this story. Shechem rapes Dinah, then Dinah's brothers trick and mass murder all the men from his city in revenge. An awful story of violence and cruelty. However, the Hebrew isn't actually as clear cut as that.

The English translation tells us that Shechem 'took her and raped her', but the original Hebrew is more ambiguous. The first word, which is translated 'took her', is the same word used when Jacob sleeps with Leah in Genesis 30:16, or when Jacob lies down to sleep in the desert in Genesis 28:11. The next word, which is translated as 'raped her', is a hard word to put into English. It is normally translated as 'violates'. It definitely can mean rape, and is certainly used that way elsewhere in the Bible. It's root word means to afflict or mishandle, but it can also mean to submit or humble oneself. In short, the word could mean rape, but it could also mean that Dinah willingly submitted to Shechem. The word is ambiguous.

Of course, the one person in the story that could say whether Shechem was guilty of rape would be Dinah herself - and yet she is never allowed to speak. She's never asked her opinion, or what her thoughts are. In fact, she's hardly mentioned in Genesis at all. We're told she was born in Genesis 30:21, and that she goes to Egypt with the rest of the family in Genesis 46:15. Other than that, this is the only story which mentions her, and she's not given a voice. She is almost completely passed over and forgotten. Was she raped by Shechem, and her brothers took bloody revenge? Did she fall in love with Shechem, only to lose him to the swords of her angry and unapproving brothers? We don't know.

This is far from the first time that women have been misused, denied a voice or sexually exploited in Genesis.

In Genesis 12 Abram tells the Pharaoh that Sarai is his sister, rather than his wife. Sarai is taken into Pharaoh's palace. In Genesis 20, Sarai, now named Sarah, is treated exactly the same way again, as her husband again claims she is his sister, this time to Abimelech the king of Gerar. Isaac is guilty of exactly the same sin, telling others that Rebekah is his sister, rather than his wife. In Genesis 19 Lot offers his own two daughters to be raped by the mob, in order to stop them raping his angelic visitors. At no point are any of the women involved given a voice or a say in what happens to them.

The story of Dinah is part of a pattern of men treating women however they see fit, without ever asking them how they feel or what their hopes are. In our story today, Dinah's family at least show some care for their sister - or at least their understanding of how their sister should be treated. However, Dinah herself is still silent and its left purposefully ambiguous as to whether she would be pleased or devastated by the result.

However, this is not the last time in Genesis that a woman will be mistreated sexually by a man.

Although in this climatic story, the woman takes charge!

Creation to New Creation

In Genesis 38 Judah's son, Er, marries a woman called Tamar. When Er dies Tamar marries his brother, Onan, only for him to die too. The custom at the time was for Tamar to then marry the youngest brother Shelah. However, in fear of his youngest sons death, Judah refuses to let the marriage take place and sends Tamar back to her parental home. It is hard for us to get our heads round just how wrong this would have been perceived to be within that culture. Without an heir, and without the prospect of marriage Tamar's future was desperate. So Tamar decides to act. She dresses as a prostitute and tricks her father-in-law into bed. Once she's discovered to be pregnant Judah gets angry only for her to reveal that he is the father. Reading this with 21st Century eyes it feels like Tamar acted wrongly. However, the readers of the time would have known exactly who was acting

> When women are given a voice and agency they can flourish and outsmart the men.

wrongly in this story - Judah. Tamar instead acts boldly to counteract her mistreatment by men and secure her future. After a book full of women being treated and denied a voice, Genesis eventually comes to the place of showing that when women are given a voice and agency they can flourish and outsmart the men.

God of the voiceless. When we are guilty of denying people a voice, remind us that you call us to empower those who have been disempowered.
Amen.

Holy Monday

26 Judah said to his brothers, 'What will we gain if we kill our brother and cover up his blood? 27 Come, let's sell him to the Ishmaelites and not lay our hands on him; after all, he is our brother, our own flesh and blood.' His brothers agreed.
28 So when the Midianite merchants came by, his brothers pulled Joseph up out of the cistern and sold him for twenty shekels of silver to the Ishmaelites, who took him to Egypt.
Genesis 37:26-28

In our journey through Lent we now enter Holy Week itself. The week in which we journey through that final week of Jesus' life. The week which will climax with the Son of God hanging on a cross before jeering crowds. The week which will lead us, ultimately, to Easter itself - the Day of Resurrection. Yesterday was Palm Sunday, the day in which Jesus rides into Jerusalem as king. The whole of Jesus' ministry has been leading up to this point. For hundreds of years the city of Jerusalem has waited for its saviour to arrive, and finally he does. But he does not come on a war horse, with armies and worldly power. Instead he comes on a donkey surrounded by cheering

Creation to New Creation

peasants. The saviour of Jerusalem arrives in a shockingly unexpected way.

In the book of Genesis we have journeyed from creation to the family of Abraham; from Abraham, through Isaac, to Jacob and finally we arrive at Jacob's sons. One of the many themes in the book of Genesis has been the danger of dysfunctional families. As we approach the end of the book, the same theme is still on full display. Jacob, having seen first hand the dangers of his parents each having a favourite child, now chooses to display the fact he has a favourite child, Joseph, by presenting him with a 'richly ornamented robe'. The famous coat of many colours. Of course, Joseph doesn't help matters as he tells his brothers that he has dreamt that they, along with his parents, will one day bow down before him. Regardless, his brothers are soon jealous and when they have Joseph alone, in a deserted place, they take their opportunity to get rid of him. At first they plan to kill him, but soon realise they can get more money by selling him into slavery. It is in this strange and unlikely way that Joseph first comes to Egypt.

> Time and again God does not come in power and splendour and might, but quietly, almost unnoticed.

Egypt is the great super power of its day. Even all these millennia later we know about Egypt - the Nile, the gods, the hieroglyphs, the Pharaoh. But like all ancient civilisations (and modern ones too!) it was always in danger of the next plague, or drought, or famine. But unknown to the Egyptians, God was sending them a

Creation to New Creation

saviour. Someone who would protect them from the coming famine. However, he enters the city not in splendour and power, but as a slave.

The saviour of Egypt entered the city as a slave. The saviour of the world entered the city on a donkey. Time and again God does not come in power and splendour and might, but quietly, almost unnoticed.

He enters our lives in the same way too. Often we don't even see. Often it's too strange and too discreet. Lent is about trying to stop long enough to notice the saviour coming among us. As we enter Holy Week itself let's make the commitment to be on the look out for the unexpected, hushed appearance of God in our midst.

God who often chooses to come not in displays of power and might, but in the secretive, soundless ways of humility. Open our eyes and minds to notice when you come among us.
Amen.

Creation to New Creation

Holy Tuesday

Now Joseph had been taken down to Egypt. Potiphar, an Egyptian who was one of Pharaoh's officials, the captain of the guard, bought him from the Ishmaelites who had taken him there.
2 The Lord was with Joseph so that he prospered, and he lived in the house of his Egyptian master. 3 When his master saw that the Lord was with him and that the Lord gave him success in everything he did, 4 Joseph found favour in his eyes and became his attendant. Potiphar put him in charge of his household, and he entrusted to his care everything he owned. 5 From the time he put him in charge of his household and of all that he owned ... Now Joseph was well-built and handsome, 7 and after a while his master's wife took notice of Joseph and said, 'Come to bed with me!'
8 But he refused. ...11 One day he went into the house to attend to his duties, and none of the household servants was inside. 12 She caught him by his cloak and said, 'Come to bed with me!' But he left his cloak in her hand and ran out of the house.
13 When she saw that he had left his cloak in her hand and had run out of the house, 14 she called her household

servants. 'Look,' she said to them, 'this Hebrew has been brought to us to make sport of us! He came in here to sleep with me, but I screamed. **15** *When he heard me scream for help, he left his cloak beside me and ran out of the house.' ...*
19 *When his master heard the story his wife told him, saying, 'This is how your slave treated me,' he burned with anger.* **20** *Joseph's master took him and put him in prison, the place where the king's prisoners were confined. But while Joseph was there in the prison,* **21** *the Lord was with him; he showed him kindness and granted him favour in the eyes of the prison warder.* **22** *So the warder put Joseph in charge of all those held in the prison, and he was made responsible for all that was done there.* **23** *The warder paid no attention to anything under Joseph's care, because the Lord was with Joseph and gave him success in whatever he did.*
Genesis 39:1-5a, 6b-8a, 11-15, 19-23

Part of my job is to plan events. Sometimes these events go brilliantly. People respond. Lives are changed. The Spirit moves. Other times ... well, not so much.

I remember spending hours and hours and hours planning and preparing a Nativity Escape Room for families. Posters had been printed and put up. Nearly 1000 leaflets had gone out into schools. Packs of resources had been put together. Everything was ready. I watched the clock in expectation. The time to begin came, and went, and I looked out on a nearly empty hall.

I suspect most of us have had that feeling. Many of us will have worked hard, given of ourselves, only for us to realise that the result wasn't what we hoped and dreamed. These could be one-off events. They could also be much more important things. Years dedicated to a spouse, only for them to up and leave. Decades given to a company only for them to make you redundant. The list could go on.

Joseph had been sold into slavery. Betrayed by his own flesh and blood. Over night he'd gone from being the favourite son to be being nothing but a slave in a foreign capital. I wonder how he felt? Sad? Angry? Desperate? No one would have blamed Joseph if he had given in to despair, or lashed out in anger at his captors.

Amazingly that does not appear to have been his reaction. Instead, Joseph seems to have accepted his new situation and reached a determination to make the best of his circumstances. In fact he works

> The only power we have is how we choose to react.

so dutifully and diligently that his new master, Potiphar, soon noticed and made him head over the entire household.

Regrettably, this happy state of affairs wasn't to last. Potiphar's wife took a shine to Joseph and when he refused to respond to her advances, she betrays him. Earlier in life his brothers had used his cloak to tell the lie that Joseph had been eaten by wild animals. Now Potiphar's wife uses his cloak to tell the lie that Joseph tried to rape her. After all his work rebuilding his life, Joseph again finds his freedom taken away. The life he has worked hard to build for himself has been taken away from him, again, through no fault of his own. This time he finds himself in prison.

Twice Joseph has been betrayed. Twice Joseph's whole life has been taken away from him. How does he respond? Joseph again knuckles down, accepts his condition and gets on with making the best of it. As such, he soon finds himself being put in charge of the whole prison.

The truth is all of us will sometimes face disappointments. Many of us will find ourselves the victims of injustice. Some of us will be betrayed. None of us have any power over what happens to us. The only power we have is how we choose to react.

Time and again Joseph faces betrayal and injustice and choses to react with grace and acceptance.

This week is Holy Week and we will soon be following Jesus through his own betrayal and injustice and, just like Joseph before him, he will respond with grace, forgiveness and acceptance.

Maybe our lesson this Holy Week is to remember that we *can* control how we choose to react. Let's make the commitment to react like Joseph, and like Jesus.

God who always responds to hate with love and to hurt with forgiveness. Help us to follow the example of your son and respond in the way of love.
Amen.

Holy Wednesday

21 They said to one another, 'Surely we are being punished because of our brother. We saw how distressed he was when he pleaded with us for his life, but we would not listen; that's why this distress has come on us.'
22 Reuben replied, 'Didn't I tell you not to sin against the boy? But you wouldn't listen! Now we must give an accounting for his blood.' 23 They did not realise that Joseph could understand them, since he was using an interpreter.
24 He turned away from them and began to weep, but then came back and spoke to them again. He had Simeon taken from them and bound before their eyes.
Genesis 42:21-24

There's no doubting that Joseph is the hero of the final section of the book of Genesis. However, as you read the story it's hard not to have questions about what Joseph is up to in regard to his actions towards his brothers.

By Genesis 42 Joseph is out of prison, and by interpreting the dreams of the Pharaoh he has become Governor of the whole land and has stored food in preparation for the famine. Jacob and his remaining sons, like everyone else, are suffering from lack of food. Jacob instructs his sons to go to Egypt and buy grain. However, he insists that his new favourite, Benjamin (Joseph's full brother, instead of half brother like the rest), stays at home. When Joseph's brothers arrive they bow before Joseph, failing to recognise him. Here is where Joseph's strange behaviour seems to begin.

Firstly, he yells at his brothers, accuses them of being spies and throws them into prison. Three days later he releases all but one of them, but tells them they can only return to Egypt if they bring their youngest brother, Benjamin, with them. After yelling earlier he breaks down weeping before sending them off. Not, however, before filling their bags both with the asked for grain, and with the silver they brought to pay for it! Joseph's brothers return to the father Jacob, only to discover that they still have their money.

Inevitably they finally need to return, even though they are terrified about what might happen. Eventually, they convince Jacob to let Benjamin accompany them. When they arrive in Egypt they are greeted and told not to worry about the silver, as the Egyptians received their payment. Joseph then orders a feast to be prepared for his brothers. Joseph again breaks down in tears. While each brother eats well, he orders that Benjamin receive 'five times as much as anyone else.' He then sends the brothers home with their grain. However, he places a silver cup in Benjamin's bag.

Once they have left, Joseph and the Egyptians give chase, find the brothers and tell them that one of them has stolen a silver cup and whoever has it will become a slave.

While the brother's protest their innocence, the cup is, of course, found in Benjamin's bag and they all head back to Egypt. Once in Egypt, Judah asks to speak to Joseph and asks to take Benjamin's place in slavery. Only at this point does Joseph reveal himself.

What exactly is Joseph doing? Why the strange games? Yelling one minute, and weeping the next. Throwing his brother's into prison, then giving them a feast. Giving them food for free, then framing them as thieves. What is going on?

I would suggest that Joseph wants to discover whether his brother's have truly repented from their actions against him all those decades ago. Firstly, he wants to see if they can admit whether they did wrong. After accusing them of spying and imprisoning them, this is exactly what they do - "Surely we are being punished because of our brother. We saw how distressed he was when he pleaded with us for his life, but we would not listen; that's why this distress has come upon us." (Genesis 42:21). It's with this admission that Joseph first weeps.

> True repentance is not just about admitting fault, it is also a commitment to act differently in the future.

However, true repentance is not just about admitting fault, it is also a commitment to act differently in the future. It seems that Joseph plans to test, given the same set of circumstances, whether his brothers would act the same. Firstly, he knows that their actions towards him came out of jealously. So he order's Jacob's new favourite son,

Creation to New Creation

Benjamin, to be brought to Egypt. Once in Egypt he treats Benjamin with special favour, feeding him more and treating him with honour. Then he gives the brothers the perfect opportunity to hand Benjamin into slavery, by planting a silver cup in his bag. However, unlike their actions with Joseph, they do not allow jealously to allow them to hand over their brother. Instead, they all mourn and Judah even asks to take his place. The brother's not only say they are sorry for what they did, they demonstrate that they are no longer the same jealous brothers they were. It is at this point that Joseph reveals himself.

All through Lent we have been looking at the sins and temptations inside of ourselves. As we come towards the climax of Lent, it is important to remind ourselves that true repentance is not just about being sorry, but also about being determined to be different from now on. May we, like Joseph's brothers, show our repentance not just with our words, but with our actions.

**God of forgiveness, when we do wrong help us not just to respond with sorrow and an admission of fault, but also with a determination to be different from now on. Wash our hearts and make them clean.
Amen.**

Maundy Thursday

8 'Judah, your brothers will praise you;
your hand will be on the neck of your enemies;
your father's sons will bow down to you.
9 You are a lion's cub, Judah;
you return from the prey, my son.
Like a lion he crouches and lies down,
like a lioness – who dares to rouse him?
10 The sceptre will not depart from Judah,
nor the ruler's staff from between his feet,
until he to whom it belongs shall come
and the obedience of the nations shall be his.
11 He will tether his donkey to a vine,
his colt to the choicest branch;
he will wash his garments in wine,
his robes in the blood of grapes.
12 His eyes will be darker than wine,
his teeth whiter than milk.
Genesis 49:8-12

Today is Maundy Thursday, the day in which we remember Jesus' last supper with his disciples. It is quite hard for us, who celebrate and commemorate the last supper every time we take communion, to grasp just how revolutionary and shocking it must have been at the time. Jesus sits down for a Passover meals with his friends. The meal which each of them would have celebrated each year from childhood. The meal which commemorated God rescuing his people from Egypt. The Passover Lamb being sacrificed, the blood painted on the door frame and the climatic plague of death sent to the Egyptians. As they go through the familiar celebration, suddenly Jesus shatters their comfortable traditions, reframing the entire meal around himself.

This is my body given for you.

This is my blood shed for you.

Even the talk of drinking blood would have been, for a Jew, more shocking than we will naturally understand. But this is nothing compared to the implications of making the passover meal about himself.

> To be a Christian is to learn to expect the unexpected.

The great act of liberation is now about Jesus!

The hero of the book of Genesis, ever since chapter 37, has been Joseph. It is through him that the family of Abraham has been saved. More than that, the promise God gave to Abraham was that all the nations of the earth would be blessed through him. In Joseph we see the very beginning of an answer to that promise. It is only through Joseph that the Egyptians, and the surrounding nations, have been saved from the devastating seven year famine. Every indication in Genesis is that the promise that was

Creation to New Creation

given to Abraham, then passed on to Isaac and Jacob is now being carried by Joseph.

In Genesis 49 as Jacob comes towards the end of his life he calls his sons to him and prays a prayer of blessing over each of them. Each son receives a specific blessing. However, the shock at the centre of the blessings is easily missed - 'The sceptre will not depart from Judah, nor the ruler's staff from between his feet, until he comes to whom it belongs and the obedience of the nations is his.' (Genesis 49:10). Despite all expectations, the person to carry the promise forward is not Joseph, but Judah.

From the beginning God has worked in unexpected and shocking ways, defying the expectations of all those who presume to know him. It is easy to go through the familiar story of Holy Week and, because we have done so many times before, fail to be shocked by the astounding way in which God chooses to save the world. As we come to the Eve of Good Friday, let's allow ourselves to be shocked afresh.

After all, to be a Christian is to learn to expect the unexpected!

God who refuses to be put into a box of our exceptions and understanding, help us to encounter the familiar stories with the shock of those who who heard them for the first time.
Amen.

Good Friday

__15__ When Joseph's brothers saw that their father was dead, they said, 'What if Joseph holds a grudge against us and pays us back for all the wrongs we did to him?' __16__ So they sent word to Joseph, saying, 'Your father left these instructions before he died: __17__ "This is what you are to say to Joseph: I ask you to forgive your brothers the sins and the wrongs they committed in treating you so badly." Now please forgive the sins of the servants of the God of your father.' When their message came to him, Joseph wept.
Genesis 50:15-17

Good Friday. The day in which Jesus dies for the forgiveness of us all.

By Genesis 50 Joseph has long been reconciled to his brothers. The whole family have moved to Egypt and resettled. Jacob has blessed both Joseph's children and his own sons. When they first came to Egypt Joseph tested their repentance and wept to discover they had changed and embraced them once again as brother's. But as Jacob's death approaches the brother's start to panic. Is Joseph just biding his time, ready to exact revenge as soon as their father is out the way? Is the forgiveness they have received real? Or are the sins of their past still going to come and get them?

With these worries buzzing around their heads they come up with a story - 'Father left instructions saying you should forgive us.'

Joseph can only weep. He already has forgiven them. It's just that they have not yet been able to forgive themselves. In his book 'The Ragamuffin Gospel', Brennan Manning tells a story. It is reported to the Archbishop that a Catholic woman is having visions of Jesus. As any Church leader will know, the line between genuine mystic and mental illness is a thin one! The Archbishop goes to see the woman and gives her instructions, 'Next time you have a vision, I want you to ask Jesus to tell you the sins that I confessed in my last confession.' Ten days later the Archbishop is informed that the woman has had another vision.

> The problem is not that they need God's forgiveness, it's that they need to forgive themselves.

"Did you do what I asked?"

"Yes, bishop, I asked Jesus to tell me the sins you confessed in your last confessions."

The bishop leaned forward with anticipation, His eyes narrowed.

What did Jesus say?"

She took his hand and gazed deep into his eyes. "Bishop," she said, "these are his exact words: I CAN'T REMEMBER."

Any church leader will also tell you that time and again they will come across people who carry their past sins around with them, like dragging a boulder on a chain. They have repented, confessed and cried out to God for forgiveness.

However, the problem is not that they need God's forgiveness, it's that they need to forgive themselves. God has already forgotten.

Like Joseph weeping to discover that his brother's are still carrying their past sins round with them when he has already forgiven them.

On Good Friday we remember Jesus dying for the forgiveness of sins. Because of what He has done, we are forgiven. We are set free.

Unless, of course, we fail to forgive ourselves.

God cannot remember your sins, do not make Jesus weep, like Joseph, by holding on to them anyway.

This Good Friday, be free.

God, who in the body of your son, died so that we all could be forgiven. Help us to accept the freedom and forgiveness you brought for us all.
Amen.

Creation to New Creation

Holy Saturday

18 His brothers then came and threw themselves down before him. 'We are your slaves,' they said.
19 But Joseph said to them, 'Don't be afraid. Am I in the place of God? 20 You intended to harm me, but God intended it for good to accomplish what is now being done, the saving of many lives. 21 So then, don't be afraid. I will provide for you and your children.' And he reassured them and spoke kindly to them.
Genesis 50:18-21

The journey of Holy Week is a familiar one for many of us. The joy of Jesus riding the donkey. The somber night of the Last Supper followed by the grief of the cross. The crowds cheering and waving palm branches at the beginning of the week and the crowds jeering for blood at the end.
Then silence.
In many ways Holy Saturday is the day in which everything is darkest. On Good Friday the shock and the fear will have carried the disciples through the day. Some hiding in corners. Others weeping in courtyards. Some even daring to stand at the foot of the cross.

But Holy Saturday is quiet. In some senses nothing happens at all. Those who had left lives, livelihoods and even family to follow Jesus now have the empty day of darkness to wonder both what happened and what was supposed to happen now.

In contrast, we finish our journey in Genesis with hope and faith. However, Joseph has certainly been through his times of darkness. At a young age, his own brothers betrayed him, coming close to killing him before they sold him into slavery. Years lived as someone else's property, climaxing with being falsely accused of rape and thrown into prison. Even in prison, he helped one man by interpreting his dream, only to, once again, be forgotten and spend yet more years without freedom.

> God is in the place of darkness and pain.

Yet at the end of Genesis, when his brother's come to him for forgiveness he is able to declare: 'You intended to harm me, but God intended it for good to accomplish what is now being done, the saving of many lives'. Whether or not Joseph was aware of it at the time, he is able to look back at those darkest, emptiest, most harrowing parts of his life and see that he was still in God's hands and in God's plan. In the same way, while the disciples must have felt abandoned and lost on Holy Saturday, the truth was that God was still working out his purpose in history.

Lent is the time in which we acknowledge the darkness and pain of life. On this last day of Lent, it is important to stop and realise that God is in the place of darkness and pain. Both the pain and hurt of Good Friday, but also the darkness and pain of Holy Saturday. The darkness of doubt. The pain of being lost. All of it is still within God's hands.

It may also be worth remembering that, just as Joseph's days in prison were followed by his days in power, so even the darkest time can come just before the time of hope and light. After all, as the saying goes, the night is always darkest before the dawn.

**God, who is with us in the times of darkness and pain, remind us that we can never be removed from your hands. Be with us in the pain of Holy Saturday, when we feel lost and confused, lift our eyes to the hope we have in you.
Amen.**

Easter Monday

*Early on the first day of the week, while it was still dark, Mary Magdalene went to the tomb and saw that the stone had been removed from the entrance ... **11** Now Mary stood outside the tomb crying. As she wept, she bent over to look into the tomb ...she turned round and saw Jesus standing there, but she did not realise that it was Jesus. **15** He asked her, 'Woman, why are you crying? Who is it you are looking for?'*
Thinking he was the gardener, she said, 'Sir, if you have carried him away, tell me where you have put him, and I will get him.'
***16** Jesus said to her, 'Mary.'*
She turned towards him and cried out in Aramaic, 'Rabboni!' (which means 'Teacher').
John 20:1, 11, 14-16

The gospel of John famously starts by echoing Genesis 1 - "In the beginning ...". From the very first verse of his Gospel, John indicates that he is writing a creation account. These echos continue in various ways through his story.

Creation to New Creation

John does not talk about miracles, but about 'signs'. Jesus turning the water into wine is labeled 'the first of his miraculous signs'. Later, Jesus heals the official's son and the gospel tells us, 'this was the second miraculous sign.' If you continue to count you would find that there are seven miraculous signs in the gospel story, followed then by the resurrection. Making Easter morning the first of the new seven.

Likewise, John has Jesus give seven 'I am' sayings - 'bread of life', 'light of the world', 'door', 'good shepherd', 'resurrection and the life', 'the way and the truth and the life' and 'vine.' He also declares 'I am' seven times e.g. 'Before Abraham was born, I am.'

The number seven, in the Hebrew world, almost always recalls creation and perfection.

> Jesus' resurrection marks the beginning of a whole new creation.

Towards the end of the gospel, Pilate brings Jesus before the crowd and declares 'Here is the man!' (Jn 19:5), echoing the creation of the man at the beginning of Genesis. As Jesus hangs on the cross he cries, 'It is finished', echoing God's words at the completion of the creation.

Now in the resurrection story Mary goes 'early on the first day of the week' to the garden, and mistakes the risen Jesus for 'the gardener'. Just as Adam tended the Garden of Eden, now the new Adam is resurrected in a garden. In these, and so many other ways, John is telling us that a new creation has burst forth.

Creation to New Creation

Jesus' resurrection marks the beginning of a whole new creation.

This, of course, implicitly presents us with a choice - which creation do you want to be part of?

The old creation, as we have seen throughout Lent, was marked with death, grief, injustice and pain. The new creation is marked with resurrection, hope, life and possibility.

Since calling Abraham, God has indicated that he wanted to renew and redeem the world. Now, through Jesus Christ, he has.

Happy Easter.

God of resurrection. We thank and praise you that through your son you have brought a whole new creation. Today we choose to live as part of this new world.
Amen.

Creation to New Creation

Easter Tuesday

Since, then, you have been raised with Christ, set your hearts on things above, where Christ is, seated at the right hand of God. 2 Set your minds on things above, not on earthly things. 3 For you died, and your life is now hidden with Christ in God. 4 When Christ, who is your life, appears, then you also will appear with him in glory... you have taken off your old self with its practices 10 and have put on the new self, which is being renewed in knowledge in the image of its Creator. 11 Here there is no Gentile or Jew, circumcised or uncircumcised, barbarian, Scythian, slave or free, but Christ is all, and is in all. 12 Therefore, as God's chosen people, holy and dearly loved, clothe yourselves with compassion, kindness, humility, gentleness and patience. 13 Bear with each other and forgive one another if any of you has a grievance against someone. Forgive as the Lord forgave you. 14 And over all these virtues put on love, which binds them all together in perfect unity.
Colossians 3:1-4, 9b-14

The truth is it can be very easy to fall into the trap of thinking of the resurrection as simply a 'happy ending' to the crucifixion. Instead, it is the beginning of a whole new creation and the invitation to a whole new way of living in the world.

Paul shockingly says that we have been raised with Christ. Not in the future, but already raised with him. Somehow, each person who puts their hope in Jesus actually shares, present tense, in his resurrection life. As Paul puts in elsewhere: 'If anyone is in Christ, the new creation has come: the old has gone, the new is here' (2 Corinthians 5:17).

This has huge consequences for how we live in the world. The old world was marked by a certain way of living. The way of striving to get ahead. Looking out for number one. My rights. My needs. However, the resurrection is an invitation to leave that way of living and embrace a new way of living in the world. Like removing one set of clothes and putting on a new set of clothes. It's about living a life marked out by kindness, unity, compassion and forgiveness.

> The resurrection is an invitation to embrace a new way of living in the world.

Paul talks about taking off our old selves and putting on the new self. In the Greek it's even more stark. Paul literally talks about taking off the old humanity and putting on the new one. In other words, the call is to enter a whole new way of being human.

The book of Genesis starts with God putting his image bearing creatures into the world. The call was to demonstrate in the world what God was like. However,

Creation to New Creation

very quickly humanity chose a different path. However, the resurrection is the beginning of the new, redeemed, restored creation and, as we have been raised with Christ, so now the call is for us to take on the role that humanity was always designed for - to reflect the image of God into the world. To clothe ourselves with the new humanity is to demonstrate what it is to be truly human.

This Easter season, let's choose to live the resurrection life, the truly human life, in the world.

God who made humanity, help us to respond to your invitation to be part of the new humanity. Help us to take off the old self and clothe ourselves with the new. Amen.

Creation to New Creation

Easter Wednesday

*Paul and Timothy, servants of Christ Jesus,
To all God's holy people in Christ Jesus at Philippi, together with the overseers and deacons:
2 Grace and peace to you from God our Father and the Lord Jesus Christ.
3 I thank my God every time I remember you. 4 In all my prayers for all of you, I always pray with joy 5 because of your partnership in the gospel from the first day until now, 6 being confident of this, that he who began a good work in you will carry it on to completion until the day of Christ Jesus.
Philippians 1:1-6*

Philippians is a letter written by a man in prison. You might, then, expect it to be full of bitterness or frustration. But you'd be wrong. Instead it is a letter brimming with thankfulness and rejoicing. It even begins with Paul offering thanks and praise for the church in Philippi. He gives thanks because of their 'partnership in the gospel'.
The word 'gospel' is the greek word '*euangelion*' (from which we get the English word, evangelical). The word has a surprising history and would have had a shocking

resonance to the people living in a Roman Colony like Philippi. In short, the word was a Roman military propaganda term. When Caesar went out on a military campaign and won a victory over a new territory, enslaving more people and crucifying those who dared to rebel, then an '*euangelion*' would be sent out across the empire. This 'gospel', or 'good news' announcement, would let everyone know that Caesar had now conquered new territory.

The early Christians took this term and applied it to Jesus and the spread of his kingdom and rule. Caesar spread his empire through violence and military might. Jesus spread his kingdom through self-sacrificial love.

Paul proclaims that the church in Philippi have partnered with him in this 'gospel'. In other words, they were actively demonstrating what it was like

> The same power who brought the universe into being is at work in all those who embrace the new world that Jesus' resurrection began.

to live under the rule of a different king. To be a part of a different empire, with different values. They were part of the new creation.

However, Paul doesn't just give thanks that they are living in a different way, but also - because he is confident that they will keep up this way of living - he declares that 'he who began a good work in you will carry it on to completion until the day of Christ Jesus.' For any first century Jew it would have been obvious what story Paul

Creation to New Creation

was echoing in this verse. In Genesis, God makes the world and declares it 'good', he then 'completes' his work. So when Paul says that God has begun a 'good' work and that he will bring it to 'completion', he's echoing the original creation story.

In other words, Paul is claiming that the same power who brought the universe into being is at work in all those who embrace the new world that Jesus' resurrection began. Paul is confident that the Christians of Philippi will be able to keep going in their work spreading the *'euangelion'* of Jesus, because the power of the creator God is at work within them.

The resurrection of Jesus is not just an invitation to live in a new way in the world. It is also the promise of the power of God within you, enabling that life to happen!

God who made the universe, when we feel powerless or overwhelmed remind us that the same power that created the universe in all its splendour is at work in us.
Amen.

Easter Thursday

Abraham 'believed God, and it was credited to him as righteousness.'
7 Understand, then, that those who have faith are children of Abraham. 8 Scripture foresaw that God would justify the Gentiles by faith, and announced the gospel in advance to Abraham: 'All nations will be blessed through you.' 9 So those who rely on faith are blessed along with Abraham, the man of faith... 16 The promises were spoken to Abraham and to his seed. Scripture does not say 'and to seeds', meaning many people, but 'and to your seed', meaning one person, who is Christ... 26 So in Christ Jesus you are all children of God through faith, 27 for all of you who were baptised into Christ have clothed yourselves with Christ. 28 There is neither Jew nor Gentile, neither slave nor free, nor is there male and female, for you are all one in Christ Jesus. 29 If you belong to Christ, then you are Abraham's seed, and heirs according to the promise.
Galatians 3:6-9, 16, 26-29

When you read through the book of Genesis it's hard to miss that Genesis 12, and the appearance of Abraham as the main character, is a huge turning point in the story. Genesis begins with creation and keeps a worldwide focus until Abraham, when it then focuses all its attention of this particular family. However, this does not mean that Genesis 1-11 doesn't fit with the rest of the book. On the contrary, Genesis 12-50 pours out of all that has gone before.

God makes a perfect world and calls his image bearing people to care for it. Unfortunately, they rebel and a downward spiral begins. Cain kills Abel. God floods the world because of its evil. The people of the world are scattered because they try and build the tower of Babel. Each time God intervenes with curses.

However, in Genesis 12 God calls Abraham (or Abram as he is then). But now, instead of cursing, he blesses. The five curses that have come before

> We have read the stories of Genesis, now we realise we are part of the same story.

are now counteracted with five blessing given to Abraham. More than that, Abraham is told that through him and his family God will bless everyone else. In other words, in Genesis 12, God begins his work of fixing his broken world. Not in the way we might expect, but through Abraham and his family (after all, God always intended to work through humans). He calls Abraham and declares that he is going to fix him and, through him, fix everyone else. Unfortunately, Abraham proved to be just as fallen as the rest of humanity. Regardless, God passes

Creation to New Creation

the promise down the family and continues to be faithful to his plan.

Here in Galatians, Paul takes that same story and tells us that the promises God made to Abraham have come true through Jesus. Jesus is the heir to the promises of Abraham, the 'seed' of Abraham. Jesus is the one through whom God has fixed his broken world, just as he always said he would.

Furthermore, Paul tells us that we have clothed ourselves with faith and so have become part of Abraham's family and, therefore, part of the promise.

This means that we are part of the same story we have been reading throughout Lent. Abraham, Isaac, Jacob, Joseph, and now us, all part of the same family, through whom God is redeeming the world!

Throughout Lent we have read the stories of Genesis, now we realise we are part of the same story. God is still fulfilling his promises. Ultimately in Jesus but, by his grace, also through us.

God of Abraham, Isaac, and Jacob, thank you that in Jesus all your promises come true. Remind us that we are now, by your grace, part of your people. Please work through us to fix your broken world.
Amen.

Easter Friday

> *13 It was not through the law that Abraham and his offspring received the promise that he would be heir of the world, but through the righteousness that comes by faith. 14 For if those who depend on the law are heirs, faith means nothing and the promise is worthless, 15 because the law brings wrath. And where there is no law there is no transgression. 16 Therefore, the promise comes by faith, so that it may be by grace and may be guaranteed to all Abraham's offspring – not only to those who are of the law but also to those who have the faith of Abraham. He is the father of us all.*
> Romans 4:13-16

Starting in Genesis 12, and then repeating regularly throughout the story, God promises to bless Abraham and through him to bless all the nations. This promise largely includes two areas.

The first is that Abraham would be the father of a huge number of descendants, as many as there are stars in the sky. In the New Testament, including in Romans 4, we are told that all those who have faith, like Abraham, become part of Abraham's family. This repeated promise in Genesis may come true in an unexpected way, but it clearly comes true.

The second part of the regularly repeated promise is that Abraham and his descendants would be given a land to possess. In many ways this promise is central to the whole Old Testament story. Moses leads the Israelites out of Egypt to go to the Promised Land. King David rules over a united Promised Land. The prophets warn that they will be removed from the land if the people don't turn to God. The people are exiled out of the land. Again and again, the story is about how the people of God are related to the Promised Land. Even today this promise has ramifications as we look at the on going political trouble in the 'Holy Land' (a heart breaking irony for an area who's capital city is called Jerusalem' - 'Jerusalem' means 'City of Peace').

> The hope of the Bible was not to escape elsewhere, but for the restoration and redemption of this world.

However, just like with the first part of the promise, the New Testament points us to a surprising fulfilment of this promise. According to Paul in Romans 4:13 Abraham 'received the promise that he would be heir of the world.' The promise that the family of Abraham would inherit the land seems to be expanded to them inheriting the whole world.

When I was growing up I was lucky enough to be brought up in a church going family. My parents were Christians

Creation to New Creation

and, without pressure or compulsion, encouraged me to explore faith myself. For whatever reason, as I was growing up I always assumed, and somehow got the message, that the Christian faith taught that our hope was to 'go to heaven' when we died. I was never very sure what this would look like, or how this would work, but that was still the understanding I had.

I still remember the shock when I first truly took in the message that actually the Christian hope was a lot more 'earthly.' That the hope of the Bible was not to escape elsewhere, but for the restoration and redemption of this world.

At Easter we celebrate that Jesus was physically resurrected, the first part of the restored, renewed creation. In Romans 4, Paul declares that the heirs of Abraham will inherit the world. When Christ returns, the whole creation will be 'resurrected' in the same way Jesus was.

Now that's a hope worth having!

**God of resurrection. We thank you that you have not given up on this broken world, but that you are committed to redeeming and restoring it. Help us to hold on to the promise we have in you.
Amen.**

Creation to New Creation

Easter Saturday

Then I saw 'a new heaven and a new earth,' for the first heaven and the first earth had passed away, and there was no longer any sea. 2 I saw the Holy City, the new Jerusalem, coming down out of heaven from God, prepared as a bride beautifully dressed for her husband. 3 And I heard a loud voice from the throne saying, 'Look! God's dwelling-place is now among the people, and he will dwell with them. They will be his people, and God himself will be with them and be their God. 4 "He will wipe every tear from their eyes. There will be no more death" or mourning or crying or pain, for the old order of things has passed away.'
5 He who was seated on the throne said, 'I am making everything new!'
Revelation 21:1-5a

Then the angel showed me the river of the water of life, as clear as crystal, flowing from the throne of God and of the Lamb 2 down the middle of the great street of the city. On each side of the river stood the tree of life, bearing twelve crops of fruit, yielding its fruit every month. And the leaves of the tree are for the healing of the nations. 3 No

longer will there be any curse. The throne of God and of the Lamb will be in the city, and his servants will serve him. 4 They will see his face, and his name will be on their foreheads. 5 There will be no more night. They will not need the light of a lamp or the light of the sun, for the Lord God will give them light. And they will reign for ever and ever. 6 The angel said to me, 'These words are trustworthy and true.
Revelation 22:1-6a

Many weeks ago we began our Lenten journey in the garden of Eden, with the tree of life and God dwelling with his people. We have journeyed through floods and famines, through family betrayals and bereavements, through dreams and angelic visits. We have walked, alongside Jesus, through betrayal and resurrection. Yet, in some strange way, we still end where we began. Back in the garden. Back at the tree of life. God back with his people.

The image at the end of revelation is a radical new beginning, and a return to where the whole journey began. Here we have the image of the whole world restored. The New Creation in all its glory and splendour. Not, as I used to mistakenly believe, an image of people 'going to heaven', but an image of heaven itself coming to earth. In the garden of Eden, God walked with his people in the cool of the day, now God is with his people again and will wipe ever tear from their eye. Everything is made new!

Notice also, just as Abraham was promised he would bring blessing to the nations, so now the leaves of the tree of life are for the healing of the nations.

Creation to New Creation

Easter is not just about the resurrection of Jesus, it is about how all the promises of God come together in him. How we are raised with him and brought into the new creation. How we are brought into the family of Abraham and promised the world as our inheritance. It's about the promise that the God of creation is working through us to bring the Kingdom of God to bear in our world. It's about how one day Jesus will return and restore and redeem this hurt and broken world. It's about hope and healing and the power of self-sacrifical love.

> Easter is about how God is 'making everything new!'

Easter is about how God is 'making everything new!'
Happy Easter to you all.

**God who makes everything new. We thank and praise you for all that you have done and all that you have promised to do. We thank you that you raised Jesus from the dead. We thank you that you work in and through us to bring that resurrection power to your world. We thank you that one day there will be a new heaven and a new earth.
Amen.**

Acknowledgements

As we come to the end of this book of reflections, I would simply like say a few 'thank yous'.
Thank you to my wonderful family. To my beautiful wife, Carole, for her support and love. To my two gorgeous and amazing daughters, Sarah and Anabel. My family make all things possible, and all things worthwhile.
I'd like to thank my Mum for her unceasing and unconditional love. My thanks also to Linda, a vital part of our family. Thank you both also for reading an early version of this book and for your feedback.
Thank you to Kathy Robertson, for being a fantastic friend and colleague. Thank you also for your feedback on an early draft of this book.
It goes without saying that any mistakes that remain are entirely my own.
I'd like to thank the fantastic people of St Catherine's and St Andrew's Churches. It is a privilege to be your vicar.
Thank you to Barbara Stephens for your wonderful art work, which you were kind enough to let me use on the front cover.
Thank you to Bishop Nick Baines for kindly agreeing to write the foreword. His generosity in taking time out of

Creation to New Creation

his busy schedule to read the book, and endorse it, is a real gift.

Finally, all praise and thanks go to my magnificent creator God.

In the unlikely event of anyone reading this book, and in the even more unlikely event of there being any profits from this book, then they will all go to the unceasing and awe-inspiring work of the St Catherine's Centre. Please consider donating.

You can give by going to https://givealittle.co/campaigns/3ef12aac-2ea1-41ce-84b9-3074ebbd4e0a or scanning the QR code below.

Finally, this little book, such as it is, is dedicated to my Dad. Word's cannot express how heartbroken I am that he died before he could read it. May he rest in peace and rise in glory.

Printed in Great Britain
by Amazon